THE
OJIBWA

(modern state and international boundaries)

Lake Winnipeg

CANADA

ONTARIO

QUEBEC

Cree

Lake Superior

OJIBWA

Ottawa

River

St. Lawrence

Sioux

Fox

Menominee

MICHIGAN

Lake Huron

Huron

MINNESOTA

Mississippi

WISCONSIN

Lake Michigan

Potawatomi

Lake Ontario

Iroquois

NEW YORK

Iowa

Sauk

River

IOWA

Lake Erie

Illinois

Miami

PENNSYLVANIA

NEW JERSEY

ILLINOIS

INDIANA

OHIO

MARYLAND

DELAWARE

NSAS

MISSOURI

Shawnee

WEST VIRGINIA

KENTUCKY

VIRGINIA

INDIANS OF NORTH AMERICA

THE
OJIBWA

Helen Hornbeck Tanner
D'Arcy McNickle Center for the History of the American Indian,
Newberry Library

Frank W. Porter III
General Editor

CHELSEA HOUSE PUBLISHERS
New York   Philadelphia

On the cover   Worn to dances and other Ojibwa ceremonies, these leggings are made from heavy, dark blue trade cloth and overlaid with a floral pattern of embroidered beadwork.

Chelsea House Publishers
Editor-in-Chief   Remmel Nunn
Managing Editor   Karyn Gullen Browne
Copy Chief   Mark Rifkin
Picture Editor   Adrian G. Allen
Art Director   Maria Epes
Assistant Art Director   Noreen Romano
Manufacturing Director   Gerald Levine
Systems Manager   Lindsey Ottman
Production Manager   Joseph Romano
Production Coordinator   Marie Claire Cebrián

Indians of North America
Senior Editor   Liz Sonneborn

Staff for **THE OJIBWA**
Assistant Editor   Leigh Hope Wood
Copy Editor   Benson D. Simmonds
Editorial Assistant   Michele Haddad
Designer   Debora Smith
Picture Researcher   Sandy Jones

5   7   9   8   6

Library of Congress Cataloging-in-Publication Data

Tanner, Helen Hornbeck.
     The Ojibwa/by Helen Hornbeck Tanner.
        p.   cm.—(Indians of North America)
     Includes bibliographical references (p.   ) and index.
     Summary: Examines the culture, history, and changing fortunes of the Ojibwa Indians.
     ISBN 1-55546-721-0
        0-7910-0392-2 (pbk.)
     1. Ojibwa Indians. [1. Ojibwa Indians. 2. Indians of North America.] I. Title II. Series: Indians of North America (Chelsea House Publishers)
                                                        90-2455
E99.C6T344   1991   CIP
970.004′973—dc20   AC

CONTENTS

INDIANS OF NORTH AMERICA

CHELSEA HOUSE PUBLISHERS

INDIANS OF NORTH AMERICA: CONFLICT AND SURVIVAL

Frank W. Porter III

The Indians survived our open intention of wiping them out, and since the tide turned they have even weathered our good intentions toward them, which can be much more deadly.

John Steinbeck
America and Americans

When Europeans first reached the North American continent, they found hundreds of tribes occupying a vast and rich country. The newcomers quickly recognized the wealth of natural resources. They were not, however, so quick or willing to recognize the spiritual, cultural, and intellectual riches of the people they called Indians.

The Indians of North America examines the problems that develop when people with different cultures come together. For American Indians, the consequences of their interaction with non-Indian people have been both productive and tragic. The Europeans believed they had "discovered" a "New World," but their religious bigotry, cultural bias, and materialistic world view kept them from appreciating and understanding the people who lived in it. All too often they attempted to change the way of life of the indigenous people. The Spanish conquistadores wanted the Indians as a source of labor. The Christian missionaries, many of whom were English, viewed them as potential converts. French traders and trappers used the Indians as a means to obtain pelts. As Francis Parkman, the 19th-century historian, stated, "Spanish civilization crushed the Indian; English civilization scorned and neglected him; French civilization embraced and cherished him."

Nearly 500 years later, many people think of American Indians as curious vestiges of a distant past, waging a futile war to survive in a Space Age society. Even today, our understanding of the history and culture of American Indians is too often derived from unsympathetic, culturally biased, and inaccurate reports. The American Indian, described and portrayed in thousands of movies, television programs, books, articles, and government studies, has either been raised to the status of the "noble savage" or disparaged as the "wild Indian" who resisted the westward expansion of the American frontier.

Where in this popular view are the real Indians, the human beings and communities whose ancestors can be traced back to ice-age hunters? Where are the creative and indomitable people whose sophisticated technologies used the natural resources to ensure their survival, whose military skill might even have prevented European settlement of North America if not for devastating epidemics and disruption of the ecology? Where are the men and women who are today diligently struggling to assert their legal rights and express once again the value of their heritage?

The various Indian tribes of North America, like people everywhere, have a history that includes population expansion, adaptation to a range of regional environments, trade across wide networks, internal strife, and warfare. This was the reality. Europeans justified their conquests, however, by creating a mythical image of the New World and its native people. In this myth, the New World was a virgin land, waiting for the Europeans. The arrival of Christopher Columbus ended a timeless primitiveness for the original inhabitants.

Also part of this myth was the debate over the origins of the American Indians. Fantastic and diverse answers were proposed by the early explorers, missionairies, and settlers. Some thought that the Indians were descended from the Ten Lost Tribes of Israel, others that they were descended from inhabitants of the lost continent of Atlantis. One writer suggested that the Indians had reached North America in another Noah's ark.

A later myth, perpetrated by many historians, focused on the relentless persecution during the past five centuries until only a scattering of these "primitive" people remained to be herded onto reservations. This view fails to chronicle the overt and covert ways in which the Indians successfully coped with the intruders.

All of these myths presented one-sided interpretations that ignored the complexity of European and American events and policies. All left serious questions unanswered. What were the origins of the American Indians? Where did they come from? How and when did they get to the New World? What was their life—their culture—really like?

In the late 1800s, anthropologists and archaeologists in the Smithsonian Institution's newly created Bureau of American Ethnology in Washington,

D.C., began to study scientifically the history and culture of the Indians of North America. They were motivated by an honest belief that the Indians were on the verge of extinction and that along with them would vanish their languages, religious beliefs, technology, myths, and legends. These men and women went out to visit, study, and record data from as many Indian communities as possible before this information was forever lost.

By this time there was a new myth in the national consciousness. American Indians existed as figures in the American past. They had performed a historical mission. They had challenged white settlers who trekked across the continent. Once conquered, however, they were supposed to accept graciously the way of life of their conquerors.

The reality again was different. American Indians resisted both actively and passively. They refused to lose their unique identity, to be assimilated into white society. Many whites viewed the Indians not only as members of a conquered nation but also as "inferior" and "unequal." The rights of the Indians could be expanded, contracted, or modified as the conquerors saw fit. In every generation, white society asked itself what to do with the American Indians. Their answers have resulted in the twists and turns of federal Indian policy.

There were two general approaches. One way was to raise the Indians to a "higher level" by "civilizing" them. Zealous missionaries considered it their Christian duty to elevate the Indian through conversion and scanty education. The other approach was to ignore the Indians until they disappeared under pressure from the ever-expanding white society. The myth of the "vanishing Indian" gave stronger support to the latter option, helping to justify the taking of the Indians' land.

Prior to the end of the 18th century, there was no national policy on Indians simply because the American nation had not yet come into existence. American Indians similarly did not possess a political or social unity with which to confront the various Europeans. They were not homogeneous. Rather, they were loosely formed bands and tribes, speaking nearly 300 languages and thousands of dialects. The collective identity felt by Indians today is a result of their common experiences of defeat and/or mistreatment at the hands of whites.

During the colonial period, the British crown did not have a coordinated policy toward the Indians of North America. Specific tribes (most notably the Iroquois and the Cherokee) became military and political pawns used by both the crown and the individual colonies. The success of the American Revolution brought no immediate change. When the United States acquired new territory from France and Mexico in the early 19th century, the federal government wanted to open this land to settlement by homesteaders. But the Indian tribes that lived on this land had signed treaties with European governments assuring their title to the land. Now the United States assumed legal responsibility for honoring these treaties.

At first, President Thomas Jefferson believed that the Louisiana Purchase contained sufficient land for both the Indians and the white population. Within a generation, though, it became clear that the Indians would not be allowed to remain. In the 1830s the federal government began to coerce the eastern tribes to sign treaties agreeing to relinquish their ancestral land and move west of the Mississippi River. Whenever these negotiations failed, President Andrew Jackson used the military to remove the Indians. The southeastern tribes, promised food and transportation during their removal to the West, were instead forced to walk the "Trail of Tears." More than 4,000 men, woman, and children died during this forced march. The "removal policy" was successful in opening the land to homesteaders, but it created enormous hardships for the Indians.

By 1871 most of the tribes in the United States had signed treaties ceding most or all of their ancestral land in exchange for reservations and welfare. The treaty terms were intended to bind both parties for all time. But in the General Allotment Act of 1887, the federal government changed its policy again. Now the goal was to make tribal members into individual landowners and farmers, encouraging their absorption into white society. This policy was advantageous to whites who were eager to acquire Indian land, but it proved disastrous for the Indians. One hundred thirty-eight million acres of reservation land were subdivided into tracts of 160, 80, or as little as 40 acres, and allotted tribe members on an individual basis. Land owned in this way was said to have "trust status" and could not be sold. But the surplus land—all Indian land not allotted to individuals—was opened (for sale) to white settlers. Ultimately, more than 90 million acres of land were taken from the Indians by legal and illegal means.

The resulting loss of land was a catastrophe for the Indians. It was necessary to make it illegal for Indians to sell their land to non-Indians. The Indian Reorganization Act of 1934 officially ended the allotment period. Tribes that voted to accept the provisions of this act were reorganized, and an effort was made to purchase land within preexisting reservations to restore an adequate land base.

Ten years later, in 1944, federal Indian policy again shifted. Now the federal government wanted to get out of the "Indian business." In 1953 an act of Congress named specific tribes whose trust status was to be ended "at the earliest possible time." This new law enabled the United States to end unilaterally, whether the Indians wished it or not, the special status that protected the land in Indian tribal reservations. In the 1950s federal Indian policy was to transfer federal responsibility and jurisdiction to state governments, encourage the physical relocation of Indian peoples from reservations to urban areas, and hasten the termination, or extinction, of tribes.

Between 1954 and 1962 Congress passed specific laws authorizing the termination of more than 100 tribal groups. The stated purpose of the termination policy was to ensure the full and complete integration of Indians into American society. However, there is a less benign way to interpret this legislation. Even as termination was being discussed in Congress, 133 separate bills were introduced to permit the transfer of trust land ownership from Indians to non-Indians.

With the Johnson administration in the 1960s the federal government began to reject termination. In the 1970s yet another Indian policy emerged. Known as "self-determination," it favored keeping the protective role of the federal government while increasing tribal participation in, and control of, important areas of local government. In 1983 President Reagan, in a policy statement on Indian affairs, restated the unique "government is government" relationship of the United States with the Indians. However, federal programs since then have moved toward transferring Indian affairs to individual states, which have long desired to gain control of Indian land and resources.

As long as American Indians retain power, land, and resources that are coveted by the states and the federal government, there will continue to be a "clash of cultures," and the issues will be contested in the courts, Congress, the White House, and even in the international human rights community. To give all Americans a greater comprehension of the issues and conflicts involving American Indians today is a major goal of this series. These issues are not easily understood, nor can these conflicts be readily resolved. The study of North American Indian history and culture is a necessary and important step toward that comprehension. All Americans must learn the history of the relations between the Indians and the federal government, recognize the unique legal status of the Indians, and understand the heritage and cultures of the Indians of North America.

A Forest Lane, *by W. H. Bartlett. According to their ancient legends, the Ojibwa Indians first lived by the Great Salt Sea in the east before following a vision that led them westward to the forests of the Great Lakes region.*

COMING
TO
THE GREAT LAKES

Before the beginning of the world, only Kitche Manido, the Great Spirit, existed. As the all-powerful Creator, Kitche Manido first made the four basic elements—rock, fire, wind, and water. From these, he fashioned the sun and stars, the Earth, and everything on it. He made the trees and plants and all forms of animal life—the four leggeds, wingeds, and swimmers. Last of all he created the two leggeds, the humans. He then organized the world by the Four Directions: Wauban (east), Shawan (south), Ningabian (west), and Keewatin (north). Two other sacred directions were the Sky above and the Earth below.

After a time, Earth had a Great Flood, and the seas washed over the land. One after another of the animals tried to dive down to find land. Finally, the humble muskrat disappeared beneath the water and after a long time returned to the surface nearly dead, but carrying a bit of soil in his paw. From this bit of dirt, Earth was re-created.

From Kitche Manido, every part of Creation received a spirit and a purpose in the Circle of Life. The plants would provide food and medicines; the trees would give shelter. The animals would sacrifice their lives to provide food and clothing for humans—the Anishinabe. But in return for everything taken from Creation, the Anishinabe knew they should give a tobacco offering and a prayer.

Kitche Manido was also responsible for Nanabush, or Wenebojo. Nanabush was born of an Earth Mother and Father Sun, so he belonged to both the earth and spirit worlds. A trickster who could change form to become other beings, animals, or even a rock, he brought all manner of knowledge to the Anishinabe. Nanabush also served as an intermediary between the Anishinabe and the spirit world. He carried the Anishinabe's messages to the Grandfathers, lesser manidos who in turn could intercede with Kitche Manido.

The Anishinabe first lived by the Great Salt Sea in the east, but long ago they followed the vision of a *megis* (cowrie shell) that led them westward to the Great Lakes. This account is part of the ancient legends of the Ojibwa Indians, which explain how they were created and how they came to live in the region of the Great Lakes. The stories embody many traditional Ojibwa values and beliefs. Among these are a reverence for the spirits, which the Ojibwa believe animate all things, and a belief in dreams and visions as a means of receiving instruction and guidance.

Since their early history, the Ojibwa have called themselves Anishinabe, meaning spontaneously created or original man. Many of them prefer this name today. The name Ojibwa may refer to their puckered moccasins but probably evolved from a mispronunciation of *o-jib-i-weg*, a term meaning "those who make pictographs." Pictographs are pictures that are used for recording information. The Ojibwa painted pictographs on birch bark, making them one of the few North American Indian groups that traditionally used a form of writing.

The Ottawa as well as the Ojibwa refer to themselves as Anishinabe. Along with the Potawatomi, the two tribes migrated from the Atlantic coast to the Great Lakes region about 500

years ago. The Indians traveled along the St. Lawrence River and then split up upon reaching the Straits of Mackinac, near the present-day city of St. Ignace, Michigan. The Ottawa journeyed to the territory north of Lake Huron; the Potawatomi traveled to what is now southwestern Michigan; and the Ojibwa settled in the region around the eastern end of Lake Superior and north shore of Lake Huron. Because of their common origin, they are still called the Three Fires.

Before the Ojibwa first encountered Europeans in the early 17th century, the Indians ranged from Michipicoten Bay to the north shore of Lake Huron and south into the upper peninsula of present-day Michigan. They visited one another by way of an extensive network of lakes and river routes. The St. Marys River, the outlet from Lake Superior feeding into Lake Huron, is a link in one of the oldest and most important water routes across the North American continent. One of the Ojibwa's main villages, Bowating (meaning "the place at the falls"), was located at the middle of this water route. Because of its accessibility and the abundant local supply of whitefish, the village became an important center for ceremonies and trade.

The population of Bowating, estimated to have been 250 to 500 in the early 17th century, increased during the summer months, when relatives and visitors arrived for trading, games, storytelling, and entertainment. These gatherings also provided an opportunity for

A section of a Midewiwin birch-bark scroll. By painting pictures on sheets of birch bark, Midewiwin members passed down sacred, ritual songs and instructions to future Mide. The Ojibwa was one of the few tribes in North America to use a form of writing to record information.

Ojibwa leaders to meet in councils to discuss war expeditions and defense strategies against their Iroquois enemies to the east and Sioux enemies to the west.

Visiting bands came from communities on the eastern shore of Lake Superior, from settlements along the south shore of Lake Superior, and from villages on the nearby Garden River.

These people grew corn, although the harvest was unpredictable in this latitude. Corn, like wild rice, was a storable crop that provided the Indians with a readily available food source, when the harvest was not damaged by frost.

The early summer gatherings at Bowating also attracted Indians from other tribes. The Huron came from the region west of Lake Simcoe on the On-

Spearing Fish in Winter, *by Seth Eastman, depicts Ojibwa fishing through ice in the district northwest of Lake Superior. Unless topped with ice too thick to penetrate, the St. Marys River provided a steady source of food all year. The Ojibwa settled on its banks and called their main village Bowating.*

tario peninsula, carrying pottery and their own surplus corn for trade. Buffalo hides from the Illinois and Miami country south of Lake Michigan, along with shells from the coast of the Gulf of Mexico, were also brought in by canoe. Among the goods that the Ojibwa could contribute to the trade were high-quality furs, copper for ornaments, birch-bark canoes, birch-bark containers of various sizes, and *kinnikinnick*, a mixture of dried plants used for smoking.

The Ojibwa, Ottawa, and Potawatomi enjoyed a particularly close trade relationship. All three groups spoke related languages that linguists classify as part of the Algonquian language family. (Almost all Indian people in northeastern North America spoke Algonquian tongues.) The members of the Three Fires also shared a similar way of life.

The Ojibwa traded with people from other language groups as well. For instance, they often dealt with the Winnebago of present-day Wisconsin, who spoke a Siouan tongue, and the Huron, who spoke an Iroquoian language. The Huron played an especially important role in early trade in the Great Lakes region. During the winters, many Indians, including the Ottawa, lived near the large Huron centers around Lake Simcoe. These palisaded towns could house two or three thousand people in long multifamily houses. From these Huron centers, traders from the Nipissing tribe carried goods to the north as far as James Bay. Beginning in the early 17th century, they met British ships there and traded with their crews. Ottawa and Huron traders met French traders on the St. Lawrence River. Then they traveled westward through the Straits of Mackinac and into Lake Michigan to barter with tribes living along Green Bay in present-day Wisconsin.

The Huron were not, however, on friendly terms with the Iroquois of northern New York, even though these tribes spoke similar Iroquoian languages and shared many of the same cultural traits. The two groups were fierce competitors, both hoping to control trade in the Northeast. In 1641, their rivalry erupted into a war that extended to the Great Lakes region. During the course of the fighting, the powerful Iroquois led expeditions westward and raided Huron settlements. The presence of the hostile Iroquois caused the Huron people to scatter. By the war's end, their people were dispersed over a wide range of territory.

Intertribal warfare, as well as other conditions that affected trade, provided opportunities for the Ojibwa to migrate. Over the course of 200 years, Ojibwa people took over territory in three waves of expansion. In the late 17th century, many moved from Bowating and their villages on the north shores of Lake Huron and traveled southeast across Ontario, Canada. In the 18th century, the Ojibwa migrated west into present-day Wisconsin and Minnesota. And in the 19th century, they journeyed beyond Lake Superior into western Canada and the United States. By the early 1840s, four main divisions of

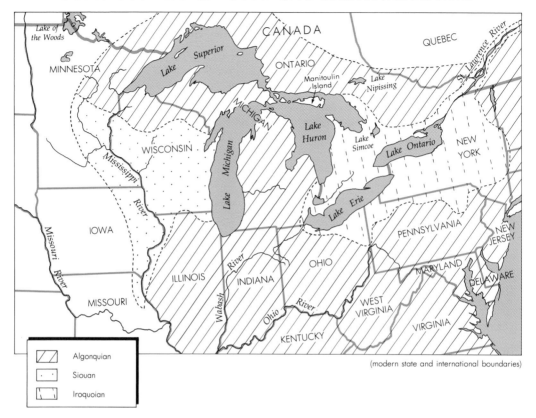

(modern state and international boundaries)

Algonquian
Siouan
Iroquoian

Ojibwa had emerged: the Southeastern Ojibwa of Southern Ontario and Michigan's Lower Peninsula (also called Mississauga or Chippewa); the Southwestern Ojibwa, who live south of Lake Superior in upper Michigan, Wisconsin, and Minnesota; the Northern Ojibwa of northern Ontario; and the Plains Ojibwa (also called the Salteaux or Bungi). Today, Ojibwa communities exist in the states of Michigan, Wisconsin, Minnesota, North Dakota, and Montana and in the Canadian provinces of Ontario, Manitoba, and Saskatchewan. About two-thirds of the 200,000 Ojibwas now live in Canada.

Present-day Ojibwa reside on more than 100 small homelands assigned to them by the Canadian and United States governments through numerous treaty negotiations. These areas are called reserves in Canada and reservations in the United States. Many other Ojibwa live in Indian communities that are not officially recognized or make their home in cities. Toronto, Ontario; Grand Rapids, Michigan; Minneapolis, Minnesota; and Winnipeg, Manitoba, all have large Ojibwa populations. Most of these urban Indians keep in contact with their non-city-dwelling kin by returning to their reserves and reservations often to visit relatives and take part in special ceremonies.

The story of the Ojibwa people is a story of adaptation to changing surroundings. Throughout the course of centuries, the Ojibwa have not only become more widespread geographically but have also grown more diverse culturally. The Ojibwa now inhabit many different regions and live in many different ways. But with each other and with their ancestors, they still share their unique identity as Anishinabe, the creations of Kitche Manido. ▲

Camping in the Forest, *by Bartlett. From the forests of the Great Lakes region, the Ojibwa collected all the materials required to construct dwellings, canoes, and containers for food.*

A CULTURE
OF
ALL SEASONS

The Ojibwa people first encountered non-Indians in their homeland in the mid-17th century. Like other Indians, they saw their way of life disrupted by these newcomers in the years following this initial contact. Many died of European diseases. Nevertheless, throughout three centuries of expansion, the Ojibwa have managed to hold on to elements of their past. Some tribe members acknowledge their rich cultural heritage through language and art. Others continue to fish and gather wild rice as their ancestors did. Consequently, the following description of the Ojibwa's traditional life in some ways describes the world of the modern Ojibwa as well.

Before non-Indians arrived, the Ojibwa followed a yearly cycle of fishing; hunting; collecting maple sap; gathering nuts, berries, and medicinal herbs; growing corn; and harvesting rice. With the change of each season, they moved to the area best suited to performing one of these necessary tasks.

At each seasonal locale, an Ojibwa family built a dwelling known as a *wigwam*. A wigwam could be constructed in less than a day with materials readily available in the woodlands. Ojibwa men first placed raw wood saplings in the ground, creating an oval measuring approximately 14 feet by 20 feet. While they pulled the saplings together in arches, women tied the framework with wood fibers. Then the family placed birch bark over the structure and covered the doorway with an animal hide. An open fireplace kept the wigwam warm and provided the family with light. With the coming of a new season, the Ojibwa rolled up the birch-bark covering and traveled to a new campsite, leaving the wood frame behind.

The Ojibwa made their own tools from bone or stone. They also manufactured bowls and ladles from wood, vessels from clay, and storage containers from bark and hide. Using wooden awls, thorn or bone needles, and moose or deer sinew, women made all of the garments worn by their family from tanned animal hides. For themselves, they sewed deerskin dresses with leggings and moccasins. For men, they fashioned breechcloths. Similar items were sewn for children out of tanned fawn hides and the skins of beaver, squirrel, or rabbit. During the winter, everyone put on heavy fur coats and lined their moccasins with rabbit fur.

Fishing was the most indispensable source of food for Ojibwa people. During the spring and fall fishing seasons, drying and smoking fish was the Ojibwa's primary occupation. Then, when families moved to winter hunting grounds, they fished through the ice. Because game animals were a source of both clothing and food, hunting was also an important task for the Ojibwa. It was not only necessary but honorable. The elders of a community invited distinguished hunters to accept leadership positions. Parents encouraged their daughters to choose a skilled fisherman or hunter for a husband.

Hunters used several methods to capture their prey. They shot waterfowl

A model of a wigwam. The Ojibwa could construct their home in less than a day by building a frame of raw wood saplings and then covering it with sheets of birch bark.

The Ojibwa placed a birch-bark bucket at the base of a maple tree to collect sap dripping from the wooden spout driven into the trunk. The process is called "tapping a tree."

In late March or early April, the Ojibwa left their hunting grounds and moved on to maple groves. There they collected sap in buckets that the women had made from birch bark specifically for this purpose. From these buckets, the Ojibwa dumped the sap into hundred-gallon moose-hide vats, in which women boiled the sticky brew into a thick syrup. After pouring the syrup into a trough, they worked it into sugar with wooden paddles. The Ojibwa had no salt, but they used this maple sugar to season their fruits, vegetables, venison, and fish.

In summer, groups of Ojibwa families gathered together near traditional berry patches and gardens, which were usually located close to a body of water suitable for fishing. Ojibwa women and children gathered, dried, and stored a variety of berries, including strawberries, raspberries, blackberries, blueberries, and wild plums. Cranberries they ate fresh. In their village gardens, they planted corn, squash, and pumpkins, which were harvested in late summer. They dried and stored part of the crop for use during the winter.

After the harvest, the village broke up into smaller groups to travel to wild rice fields. The men and women usually worked together to gather the rice. Men used a wooden pole to navigate birch-bark canoes through the shallow lakes of the rice beds. Women reached over the sides of the canoe, grabbed the wild grass growing in the water, and beat it with a stick to knock the rice into the boat. After filling the canoe, they

with bows and arrows. They caught small animals, such as beaver, mink, and fox, in traps or snares. Deer and other large game were driven into fenced-in areas, where they could be easily speared. To catch bears, Ojibwa hunters built deadfalls—traps constructed so that a heavy weight, such as a log, would fall on any animal that lumbered into them.

Indian Sugar Camp, by Eastman. After collecting sap from maple trees, the Ojibwa boiled the sticky fluid in great vats and then worked it into sugar. Having no salt on hand, the Ojibwa used this maple sugar to season their food.

headed to the shore and dried the rice kernels on flat rocks or sheets of birch bark.

Canoes were essential items to the Ojibwa. Every family owned several, each weighing from 65 pounds to 125 pounds. Covering the frame and sealed with spruce or pine gum were sheets of birch bark, an indispensable material in the Ojibwa economy. It was tough, light, and easy to peel from the tree in early spring.

After gathering rice, the Ojibwa moved on. They hunted ducks for a few months; and then in late autumn the seasonal cycle began again, with families heading to their winter hunting ground.

Having a fairly loosely structured society, the Ojibwa relied on clans to provide important social ties. An Ojibwa clan consisted of a group of people who were related through their fathers' ancestry. The bond among members of a clan was very tight. In fact, clan members were considered to be so closely related that they were not allowed to marry each other. Each clan had an animal symbol called a totem. Important totems for the Ojibwa are the Crane, Loon, Bear, Marten, and Caribou (or Reindeer).

Ceremonies were a vital component of Ojibwa life. They were performed for many different occasions, but all began with the smoking of the Pipe of Peace.

This activity has great meaning even to-day, because tobacco is a sacred substance to the Ojibwa. It represents all possible Ojibwa relationships—with Kitche Manido, other humans, animals, and plants.

The pipe was also smoked at other important events, such as intertribal councils or the inauguration of tribal chiefs. The elders of the Ojibwa were responsible for selecting leaders. When they chose someone to lead the people, they offered him the pipe. If he smoked the pipe, he accepted the responsibility.

An Ojibwa chief had relatively little power. Usually only three to four hundred people lived under his rule. He was obliged to discuss all decisions concerning his people at a council, to which all adult men and women were invited. An Ojibwa leader was expected to call councils only on occasion. To speak too frequently would cause him to appear shallow and would jeopardize his authority.

No single person presided over the entire Ojibwa tribe. Matters that concerned all of the people, such as rela-

A drawing made by Eastman, around 1850, showing Ojibwa women with a male paddler harvesting wild rice in Wisconsin. Because it could be dried and stored, rice was always a readily available food source for the Ojibwa.

tions with other tribes, were settled by a council of chiefs and principal elders of various communities.

Usually, civil chiefs were devoted to keeping peace. Military campaigns were instigated by war chiefs. Any man could be war chief. He needed only to convince warriors to join him in battle. As a rule, war chiefs were accomplished warriors, for they had to be able to cite a large number of both battles won and enemy casualties inflicted under their leadership in order to persuade other fighters to follow them. Warriors were free to accept or to reject an invitation of a war chief, but once they smoked his War Pipe they were bound to follow him into battle. During the fighting, if casualties were too high or if the war party was defeated, the war chief would lose his authority and following.

Although the elders recognized that warriors were necessary to the defense of family and community, they usually counseled young men against going to battle. They considered warring a dangerous way of showing courage and of testing strength and skill. Also, it was felt that warriors instigated bad feeling, perpetuating the spirit of vengeance. Only in times of crisis did the elders allow a warrior to lead a community. But after the crisis passed, they always forced him to relinquish his position of authority.

The elders were extremely important members of Ojibwa society. They were involved not only in advising adults but also in educating the children. Through stories, dances, songs,

Ojibwa Chief Wa-em-boesh-kaa, painted by C. McKenny. The Ojibwa selected as leaders men whom they trusted and respected. Leaders exerted their personal influence but could not command obedience.

and chants, they taught youngsters Ojibwa customs. In this way, the elders hoped to increase children's wisdom and understanding, a mission that was considered just as important as teaching practical skills, such as fishing, hunting, sewing, and cooking.

Ojibwa children received their education in three stages. When they were very young, they were cared for by the women and elders of their community. After boys turned seven, their instruction was taken over by the men, who taught male youths how to hunt and fish. Girls remained with their mothers and elders, who showed them how to make rush and birch-bark mats, clean their dwelling, take care of younger siblings, prepare hides, and make baskets. Just as hunting was part of a boy's education, these domestic duties prepared a girl for adulthood.

A girl was not considered a woman until after her first menstruation, however. The Ojibwa believed that at this time a girl received a gift from the Creator, one that was denied to men. For the duration of her period, she was lodged away from the village in a special shelter. During this time, she abstained from eating and saw only her mother or grandmother. When she returned to the village, she was thereafter treated as a woman, capable of conceiving and giving birth.

The last stage of a girl's or boy's education began when the youth asked a wise elder for guidance. The Ojibwa believed that elders should be not only knowledgeable but also wise, patient, and generous. Special instruction was given to boys or girls chosen to study herbal medicine. However, the Ojibwa believed that the power to heal was a gift that could not be learned. Medicine men and women, called *Mide*, invited candidates who already showed evidence of possessing the gift of healing to join their ranks.

The *Midewiwin*, or Grand Medicine Society, promoted health thorough balanced living, herbal medicine, and the vision quest, a ritual in which an individual went on long vigils out-of-doors without food or water with the goal of having visions, or revelations. A person had to undergo a long apprenticeship before being inducted into the Midewiwin. Apprentices received instruction from tutors who supervised the Ojibwa's accumulation of knowledge about the healthful properties of plants and the methods of preparing medicines. They also learned the prayers and songs that invoked the power of the plant medicines.

After a year of study, an apprentice was ready for an examination and initiation into the society. As part of the preparation for the event, the prospective inductee presented gifts to the tutor and also retired to a special lodge to meditate and fast as a means of purifying the mind and body.

As with all formal occasions, the initiation ceremony began as the Pipe of Peace was passed around to all present. At the proper moment, the initiate was brought to the *Midewigaan* (Medicine Lodge), which was constructed with doors facing east and west and with an opening at the top to let in light, sound, and air. Inside was placed a newly cut cedar pole, which symbolized the tree of life. Near it, a small fire was lighted.

At the eastern entrance of the Midewigaan, the initiate was met by four bear figures symbolizing the good aspects of life. In a ritual drama of drumming and songs, the bears circled the interior of the lodge, encountering four other bears who represented the temptations and obstructions to good living that the Midewiwin candidate would face.

Photographed in 1910 by Robert G. Beaulieu, an Ojibwa chief stands outside a Medicine Lodge on White Earth Reservation in Minnesota.

The most important part of the ritual was the initiate's symbolic death and rebirth as a new person. At this point the initiate was "shot" with a sacred shell, or megis, and fell motionless to the floor. With the breath of life, the presiding Mide leader revived the person. The initiate was then given an animal-skin bag to be used as a medicine bundle. The bag was to be filled with objects imbued with the inductee's spiritual power. In return, the initiate presented gifts to all the members of the society. Next, a storyteller would recount the history of the Anishinabe. When the initiation was completed, all the participants left the Midewigaan by the western door.

Members of the Midewiwin acted as both spiritual leaders and healers. The entire ceremony initiating a newcomer into the Midewiwin society was regarded as a celebration of the gift of plant knowledge received from the Creator. With plants, a Mide could heal ailments.

A new member was recognized as a first-degree member of the Midewiwin, qualified to conduct funeral services and preside at the Feast of the Dead, an annual memorial ceremony held for those who had died during the previous year. When an Ojibwa died, a period of mourning was observed after the burial. The body was placed upon a platform. It remained there for four days, during which time the spirit was thought to leave the corpse and travel to the afterworld. Then the body was wrapped in birch bark and buried with the feet pointing westward. Interred with the corpse were personal possessions, such as a medicine bundle or a weapon that had been owned by the deceased. The grave was marked with the person's clan totem, turned upside down to indicate death. Small wooden "spirit houses" were often erected over Ojibwa graves. The interment of the deceased was accompanied by an offering of food and was directed by a member of the Midewiwin society. After one year, family members were released from mourning by taking part in a feast.

In the following autumn, the Ojibwa observed the Feast of the Dead, a remembrance of all who had died within the past year. Each family that had survived a death in that time held a banquet for the entire village. At the feast, a place was set for the deceased, whose spirit was believed to remain in the family. Everyone who came dined in honor of the family and in memory of the dead.

In order to conduct other rituals, new members of the Midewiwin had to master new duties, learn more about medicine, and go on an annual retreat devoted to fasting and prayer to renew spiritual force. Today there are four degrees of Mide instruction, though in

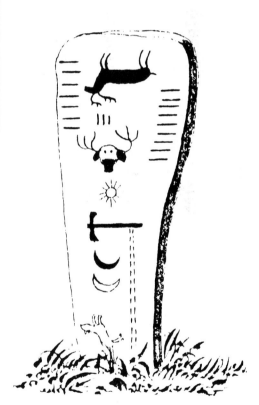

This drawing represents the totem that was placed upside down at the grave of Waubojig (White Fisher), a La Pointe leader and member of the caribou clan who died around 1793. The symbols of the arrow and pipe denote his influence in war and peace.

An Ojibwa burial ground at Lac Courte Oreilles Reservation in Wisconsin. The Ojibwa often interred personal possessions with the deceased and covered the grave with a small wooden "spirit house."

earlier times there were as many as eight. At the third degree, a member could become a *Jeesekeed*, a person able to summon supernatural powers for curing and to create unusual vibrations. Demonstrations of this ability have often been called the shaking-tent ritual.

The Midewiwin is not a society specific to the Ojibwa people. The medicine society has been active among other Great Lakes people, such as the Ottawa, Potawatomi, Menominee, Winnebago, Sauk, Fox, and Kickapoo. The Midewiwin remain an influential aspect of Ojibwa life in the 20th century. However, most of the ancient birch-bark scrolls recording the Mide songs and the history of the Anishinabe have disappeared, and few people retain the knowledge of plant medicine.

Ceremonies became especially important in unifying the Ojibwa people, not only because families within a village were separated from one another during the winter months but also because Ojibwa villages eventually became dispersed over a great range of territory. A celebration brought the Ojibwa people together, but trade gave them reason to make contact with other peoples, Indian and non-Indian alike. This contact deeply affected the Ojibwa culture. ▲

A 19th-century engraving representing Jacques Cartier exploring the St. Lawrence River. After hearing highly favorable reports about the riches of the northeastern coast of North America, fishermen ventured to the Gulf of St. Lawrence, where the waters were bountiful and the Indians were eager to trade their furs for European goods.

TRADING
WITH THE
FRENCH

European explorers who visited the northeastern coast of North America during the 16th century returned to their countries with promising reports of rivers teeming with fish and Indians eager to trade furs for manufactured goods. The international market for otter, marten, beaver, fox, mink, wolf, and bear pelts seemed unlimited. Soon the Gulf of St. Lawrence was overrun with fishermen, and Indians in the Northeast were trading furs to these Europeans for knives, hatchets, fishhooks, and needles.

Realizing that these metal goods were more durable than their own stone tools and utensils, the Indians began to vie for exclusive rights to trade furs for non-Indian goods. Thus fighting between Indian tribes increased. The trade wars spread westward as more and more Indian peoples came to desire and eventually to rely upon European goods.

In the Northeast, the Iroquois and the allied Ottawa and Huron emerged as the two principal Indian competitors in the early-17th-century fur trade. The French were the first to introduce these Indians to European trade goods, beginning about 1610. Canoes carried trade items up the St. Lawrence and Ottawa rivers to Lake Huron and to Ojibwa country. In 1614, Dutch merchants established a base for trade near present-day Albany, New York, and began trading with the Iroquois. Later, the Iroquois obtained pelts by attacking and raiding other tribes. The Huron, who lived in present-day Ontario, became middlemen in the fur trade. They traded corn to Algonquian-speaking Indians to the north and west in exchange for pelts, which they carried to the French trading center at Montreal to trade for European items. Through trade with the Huron, the Indians living in the upper Great Lakes region acquired metal goods long before Europeans came into their territory.

The fur trade was so lucrative that French explorers and traders soon started to travel west in order to deal with these Indians directly. Missionaries, soldiers, and unlicensed traders quickly followed. In early September 1641, during a Feast of the Dead celebration, several Ojibwa visitors met French Jesuit missionaries living at a Huron settlement on Georgian Bay. The Ojibwa asked the priests to visit their own village on Lake Superior. Later that month, Fathers Charles Raymbault and Isaac Jogues arrived at Bowating, which they called Sault Ste. Marie. The Ojibwa at Bowating, who were thereafter referred to by the French as Saulteurs (People of the Rapids), invited the two missionaries to live with them as brothers.

Raymbault and Jogues did not remain among the Ojibwa, but other Jesuit missionaries came to the interior to convert the Indians to Christianity. The Ojibwa, however, resisted these efforts. The Indians very much wanted to trade with these men, but they were not interested in changing their religious practices.

French officials were likewise eager to increase trade between their countrymen and Indians of the interior. However, they failed to develop trade opportunities with the Ojibwa for nearly 20 years after Raymbault and Jogues had arrived at Sault Ste. Marie. During this period, the fighting between the Iroquois and the Huron in-

creased, especially after 1640, when the Dutch began issuing firearms to Iroquois warriors. As long as the Indians fought with traditional weapons—bows and arrows, war clubs, and stone tomahawks—the death rate remained relatively low. Bullets, however, could kill more people more quickly. Therefore, the introduction of guns into the trade wars caused the number of casualties to escalate dramatically. Adding to the tragedy, the introduction of firearms came at a time when both the Huron and the Iroquois had already been decimated by epidemics. Smallpox and other diseases brought into the country by Europeans reduced their populations by about half.

By 1650, the Iroquois had destroyed the Huron villages on Georgian Bay, and the survivors scattered to other regions. Some were assimilated into the Iroquois tribes. Others followed missionaries to a refuge at Lorette, near the city of Quebec. Still other refugees fled to Christian Island in Lake Huron, where many died of disease and starvation. Those who survived fled in stages to the upper Mississippi River, accompanied by some of their Ottawa allies.

Meanwhile, Iroquois war parties moved into the Great Lakes territory, reaching the St. Marys River, below Sault Ste. Marie, in the early 1660s. With the destruction of the Huron trade network, French traders had no choice but to go to Lake Superior and trade directly with the tribes living there. Two traders, Médard Chouart, Sieur des

An Indian village on the St. Marys River. After arriving at Bowating in 1641, Jesuit missionaries named the Ojibwa village Sault Ste. Marie and called the Indians who lived there Saulteurs (People of the Rapids).

Groseilliers; and Pierre Esprit Radisson, set off in their canoes from Quebec and arrived at Chequamegon Bay in the fall of 1659. In this somewhat deserted area, they stored the bulk of their trade goods before making a winter trek to the Ottawa camp at Lac Courte Oreilles. When they returned to Quebec in early 1660, their canoes were loaded down with furs.

Radisson and Chouart's good luck did not last. The traders did not have the trading licenses that the French government required, and therefore their cargo was confiscated by the French governor. Nevertheless, their experience inspired other traders to venture west. By 1665, many Ottawa, Ojibwa, and refugee Huron were living at Chequamegon Bay. The village had become a center for trade as well as a refuge from enemy war parties.

In 1662, Ojibwa living west of Sault Ste. Marie routed the Iroquois at a place now known as Point Iroquois on Whitefish Bay. Not knowing how close to the enemy they were, an Iroquois war party had camped 15 miles above Sault Ste. Marie. Someone in a nearby Ojibwa camp saw the smoke from the Iroquois fires. After electing a chief, the Ojibwa set out in the direction of the smoke and discovered the Iroquois encampment. They returned to their own camp and organized a war party, which included Nipissing and other Indians who had left their own homes in fear of the Iroquois raids.

The party journeyed to the Iroquois camp and slipped into a nearby cove to wait for the first light of day. At dawn, they attacked. The Iroquois, still sound asleep, were completely surprised and unable to reach their weapons before the onslaught. Iroquois scouts, who had been sent out to investigate camp fires in the north, returned to discover that every member of the camp had

been killed. They returned to their own country in the east with news of the slaughter. The battle marked the last Iroquois expedition to the upper Great Lakes.

With the Iroquois threat out of the way in their home country, the Ojibwa expanded westward, hunting in territory along the south side of Lake Superior. By the end of the 17th century, they had forced the Fox to vacate the headwaters of the St. Croix River and to move farther south in present-day Wisconsin. At the western end of Lake Superior, they ousted the Sioux from what is now northern Minnesota. Within this newly acquired territory, the Ojibwa settled on Madeline Island,

Combat between the Ojibwa and the Sacs and Foxes on Lake Superior, *by Eastman. As the Ojibwa expanded westward in the late 17th century, they forced the Fox to vacate the headwaters of the St. Croix River and ousted the Sioux from what is now northern Minnesota.*

which became an important center for Ojibwa activity in the early 18th century.

Meanwhile, French officials in Quebec took measures to strengthen their influence in and control of the region around Lake Superior. As yet, no permanent trading post existed on Lake Superior. The nearest post was located at Sault Ste. Marie. The Ojibwa had to deal with Ottawa middlemen, negotiate with adventurous, unlicensed French traders known as *coureurs de bois*, and travel long distances in order to trade their pelts legally to French merchants.

In June 1671, 14 tribes of the upper Great Lakes attended a council at Sault Ste. Marie. There French nobleman Simon-Francis Daumont, Sieur de St. Lusson, proclaimed the French presence in interior North America in a dramatic pageant. By the end of the decade, another Frenchman, Daniel Greysolon, Sieur de L'hut, advanced to the western end of Lake Superior. After wintering at Sault Ste. Marie in 1678, he and his party moved westward and built a trading post at Fond du Lac. He went on to build more forts and to make alliances with various tribes.

During this same period, French traders arrived at Ojibwa communities and other neighboring Indian villages on Lake Superior to organize the collection and transport of furs to the Montreal market. Initially, the French traders were prohibited from participating in hunting and other community activities because they were not related to the Ojibwa. But as time passed,

A coureur de bois *drawn by Frederic Remington. The Ojibwa often dealt with these unlicensed French traders, as well as with Ottawa middlemen, to save themselves the long, dangerous journey to French trading posts.*

hundreds of young Frenchmen married Ojibwa women and were incorporated into the tribe. Some Ojibwa even created a special clan for their new French kin.

In 1680, the Hudson's Bay Company, a British fur-trading firm, built posts on James Bay and Hudson Bay, attracting Indians from northern Ontario and beyond. Competition between the French and the British intensified, sometimes leading to armed conflict. By the end of the 17th century, the French had captured several of these British posts, which were later returned by treaty. The British also took over the Dutch trading post near Albany, New York, and consequently increased their influence among the Iroquois.

The Iroquois continued to raid villages, blockade rivers, and attack individual canoes. In the 1680s, their Indian enemies in the Great Lakes region joined in an alliance with the French to drive the Iroquois back to their homeland in present-day New York. Not until the end of the century, however, did the Ojibwa and their Indian and French allies invade Iroquois territory and actually defeat their opponent.

Because Huron middlemen were no longer in business at this time, the French made greater attempts to develop the fur trade around Lake Superior. With this purpose in mind, Pierre Le Sueur came to Chequamegon Bay in 1693. After he built the first permanent settlement on Madeline Island, called Fort La Pointe, the Lake Superior fur trade boomed. The prosperity did not last, however. So many pelts were traded that the market was glutted and the price of furs plummeted. To limit the trade in furs, the French government suspended legal trade at all western posts by 1698.

The Ojibwa continued to expand their territory, taking over Iroquois set-

tlements that had been established in the 1660s on the north shore of Lake Ontario as bases for hunting, trading, and raiding expeditions into the north country. By the 1690s, all of these towns were occupied by Ojibwa bands from the north shore of Lake Huron and called "Mississauga" villages. (Some of the Ojibwa bands who settled in the area had traveled from the vicinity of the Mississagi River.)

The Mississauga, concentrated on the rivers in the district of present-day Toronto, prospered in their new location. The sites on rivers entering Lake Ontario provided an ample source of fish; gardening conditions were better than in the old northern settlements; and communication with neighboring bands and once-distant allies was easier. Trained runners acted as messengers. They followed paths along the ridges where forests were less dense, often traveling about 50 miles in a day. A run from present-day Toronto to Detroit required about eight days but was not considered a long trip.

The Mississauga war parties journeyed in canoes as far south as the southern Appalachian mountains of Cherokee territory. In a northerly direction, they went along a much-traveled canoe route across the neck of the Ontario peninsula to the Straits of Mackinac. The route originated on the Humber River with a portage of several miles to the South Holland River, draining into Lake Simcoe and flowing to Matchedash Bay at the south end of the larger Georgian Bay. In the Toronto dis-

A 19th-century woodcut of British fur traders at a post on Hudson Bay. After Indians from northern Ontario and beyond began to flock to the Hudson's Bay Company's newly built posts in the interior country of North America, competition between the French and the British intensified.

trict, the Mississauga became known as the Credit River band, taking their name from the river where they received supplies on credit from traders each fall with the promise to pay the following spring with proceeds of the winter hunt.

The trade wars, which had ravaged the Great Lakes for most of the 17th century, finally ended in 1701. Peace for all contenders was accomplished after preliminary arrangements had been made by the Huron and the Ottawa, representing the western Indian allies, and the Seneca and the Onondaga, representing the Iroquois Confederacy. The British held conferences with the Indians at Albany; and the French, at Montreal.

The critical problem was, of course, coming to an agreement regulating trade that would satisfy all the Indian peoples involved. The solution was to allow the Iroquois to continue to hunt in the old Huron country north of Lake Ontario and, because French trade had been officially suspended, to permit the Ottawa to freely cross Iroquois territory to trade with the English at Albany. The final council, held under French auspices in Montreal, brought together representatives of 15 Indian nations.

Despite the official declarations of peace, the trade wars left a permanent

An early-18th-century print of Quebec, the capital of New France. Because the French suspended all legal trade at western posts by 1698, the Ojibwa developed stronger ties to unlicensed French traders, who took their goods to trading houses in Montreal, Quebec, or Three Rivers.

impression in the legends of the Anishinabe peoples. Their name for all members of the Iroquois tribes had become *Nadowa*, meaning "enemy" or "snake." Likewise, the peace did not settle the daily living problems of the Ojibwa, who still had difficulty securing the European goods to which they had become accustomed. Because warfare had severely disrupted trade and because dealings at western trading posts had been prohibited, the Ojibwa living far from Montreal and Albany were particularly short of supplies. Around Lake Superior and northern Lake Huron, Indian people had either to travel the still hazardous route through Iroquois country to reach Albany or to go north to trade at British posts belonging to the Hudson's Bay Company.

Although Frenchman Antoine de la Mothe Cadillac built a new post, Fort Ponchartrain du Détroit (Detroit), in 1701, the French forts for licensed trade did not reopen until after 1715. During the intermediate period, the Ojibwa developed stronger ties with the Ottawa and illegal French traders, the coureurs de bois, who continued to make regular trips back to French trading houses in Montreal, Quebec, or Three Rivers on the St. Lawrence River. At the southern end of the expanding Ojibwa country, after peace was assured, the Mississauga found trade to be easiest with the Iroquois.

By the early 18th century, Ojibwa culture had undergone an extraordinary transformation. Men had ceased to hunt solely for immediate needs. They now trapped more animals than ever before in order to trade for metal implements, such as hatchets, knives, traps, kettles, awls, and needles; colorful blankets and clothing; and, of course, firearms. Over time, the Ojibwa became not merely accustomed to European items but depended on them. When Captain Paul le Gardeur, Sieur de Saint Pierre, came to Madeline Island in 1718 to reconstruct a trading post there, after 20 years of suspended legal trade, he found that the Indians were starving and that their overall living conditions were poor. They had abandoned and forgotten their traditional ways of making weapons, tools, and utensils from stone, bone, and wood.

European influence had altered the Indians' way of life to such an extent that the Ojibwa were no longer economically self-sufficient. Moreover, the need for European material goods perpetuated intertribal rivalry and warfare and drew the Ojibwa and many other Great Lakes Indians into new territory, causing further dispersion of individual tribes. ▲

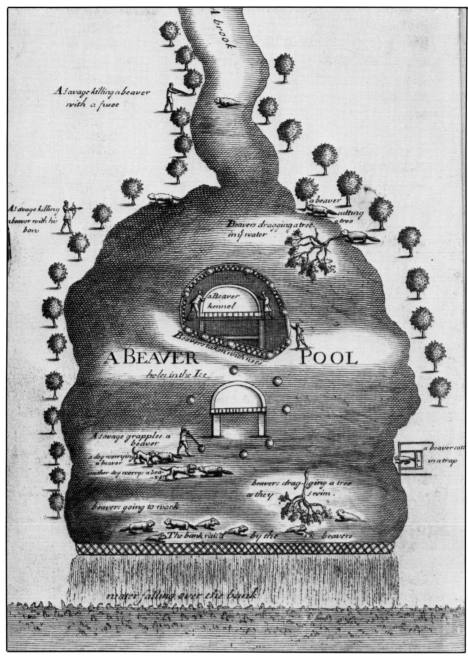

An 18th-century engraving of a beaver pool. Indians used a variety of methods to capture beavers, including guns, traps, and digging out beaver lodges. When an area in which they hunted became nearly depleted of its fur-bearing wildlife, the Indians searched for new hunting grounds.

FIGHTING OFF
COMPETITORS

In the early 18th century, the Indians of the Great Lakes continued their search for rich hunting grounds and profitable trade alliances. Their increased material needs not only led them into new lands but also drew them into many new intertribal wars.

When Cadillac built Fort Ponchartrain du Détroit in 1701, he invited Indian people from the upper Great Lakes to live in the region. He was interested in moving trade in the direction of the Ohio River, and the Indians were seeking a safe, accessible post at which to trade their pelts. Now that a fortified post had been erected on land that was left virtually untouched by hunters during the previous decades of warfare, the Indians accepted Cadillac's invitation.

Some Huron and Ottawa traveled to the area and joined other Indians already living along the Detroit River. Some Potawatomi, moving east of their usual territory in southern Michigan, established two villages south of the French fort. Among the other tribes settling in the region were a group of Mississauga who established their base on islands in the delta of the St. Clair River, the channel from Lake Huron to Lake Erie. From the St. Clair River and Lake St. Clair, the growing Mississauga spread eastward along the Thames River in Ontario and westward along the Black River and the streams flowing into Lake St. Clair. By the middle of the 18th century, these eastern Ojibwa were the dominant population of the Saginaw Bay and the "Thumb" district of southeastern Michigan.

After moving near Detroit, the Great Lakes Indians became embroiled in bitter intertribal warfare, and the French were forced to take sides. The commandant at Detroit took an Ottawa chief into French protection after Ottawa warriors attacked the Miami in 1706. Within two years the Miami had relocated south of Detroit, at the head of the Maumee River.

Then, in 1711, aided by French and tribal allies, the Huron and Ottawa attacked the large delegation of Fox Indians who had only recently settled in the Detroit area. Although the surviving Fox returned to the safety of present-day Wisconsin, the slaughter of their kin remained in their memory, and further conflict ensued in the western Great Lakes. In addition to making the waterways unsafe for their French and Indian enemies, the Fox threatened to ally themselves with the British. With the intention of completely annihilating their embittered enemies, the French retaliated. By the end of the Fox Wars, in about 1740, the Fox had deserted the Green Bay area in what is now Wisconsin.

The French had begun to push westward from the upper Great Lakes region, focusing their efforts on finding a route to the Pacific Ocean. By 1734, they had penetrated lands occupied by Cree, Assiniboin, and Ojibwa hunting bands. At Rainy Lake and Lake of the Woods, the French built trading posts and opened trade with the Cree. The Sioux, who had been at war with the Cree and Assiniboin, were greatly annoyed by this new arrangement and attacked French traders near Lake of the Woods on the northern border of present-day Minnesota.

Since 1679, the Sioux had been engaged in a profitable alliance with the Ojibwa at Lake Superior. Ojibwa middlemen carried French trade goods to Sioux villages and camps as far as 150 miles to the west, then returned to La Pointe on Chequamegon Bay with bundles of furs to be transported to Montreal. However, when the Sioux chose to attack the French in 1736, the Ojibwa broke with the Sioux and allied themselves with the Cree.

The fighting between the Ojibwa and Sioux took place all along the upper Mississippi Valley and the district adjoining the St. Croix River on the present-day Wisconsin-Minnesota border. Continuing well into the middle of the 19th century, the conflict resulted in an expansion of Ojibwa territory into what is now Wisconsin and Minnesota. At Thunder Bay, Rainy River, and Rainy Lake, the Ojibwa established new villages from which they could launch attacks against the Sioux. The Ojibwa then steadily dislodged the Sioux from their homeland in northern Minnesota. Sandy Lake, at the end of the St. Louis River portage, was one of the first Sioux bases acquired. By the 1740s, the Ojibwa had also driven the Sioux from the Lac Courte Oreilles and Lac du Flambeau districts and had established their own villages there. By the 1750s, they had forced the Sioux to evacuate Mille Lacs, Cass Lake, Winnibigoshish Lake, and Red Lake. However, they did not gain a secure hold on Leech Lake until about 1780.

These new Ojibwa settlements were located far from Chequamegon Bay, where hunting bands had been returning each year to trade and to participate in ceremonies such as the Midewiwin rite. Because many Ojibwa began to live too far away to return to Chequamegon annually and join in these activities, the occupation of new territory worked to disrupt the Ojibwa's clan and ceremonial ties with one another. Some Ojibwa were now closer to the trading posts at Rainy Lake and Lake of the Woods and ceased visiting tribespeople at Chequamegon Bay altogether.

Rivalries between French and British traders also influenced tribal migration. The Indians who moved to Detroit entered growing competition between these Europeans over control of the Indian trade in present-day Pennsylvania, Ohio, and Indiana. The struggle, which began in the Great Lakes district in the 1680s, broke into armed conflict by the mid-18th century. At this time, the principal tribes living in the Ohio Valley were the Huron, the Shawnee, the Delaware, and the Miami; but the Ojibwa and the Ottawa from the region around Detroit, the Straits of Mackinac, and the St. Marys River also became involved in the battle.

Although the various Indian tribes involved aligned themselves with either the British or the French, their objective in this warfare was to secure a supply of European goods and to protect their hunting grounds, not to ensure the hegemony of their European ally. For instance, some Ojibwa supported an uprising organized in 1747 by one group of Ohio Huron against the French because the British offered better prices for furs.

The Ottawa at Saginaw Bay took part in the attack that killed three French traders in the Illinois country during the summer of 1747. They were joined by Ojibwa from Bois Blanc Island near Mackinac Island. The attack proved unsuccessful, and most of the Ottawa at Saginaw left the area. Some of them returned to the Michilimackinac region, and others joined the Ottawa village at Detroit.

Because the British lacked easy access to the Lake Superior area and because the Indians were unable to travel to distant British posts, the French soon regained their influence over the Ojibwa and other Great Lakes Indians. Also, the Indians began to view the war as a conflict between French fur-trading interests and the British settlers' desire for land. The Iroquois had been selling land that once belonged to the Delaware and Shawnee, two tribes under Iroquois protection. As a result, the Delaware and the Shawnee were forced to withdraw to new territory west of the Appalachian Mountains. Then the Iroquois granted British land speculators rights to land in the Ohio River country, and settlers started coming across the mountains in 1754. The Delaware and the Shawnee attacked them.

As conflict between the French and British escalated, the Delaware, Shawnee, Ojibwa, and Ottawa joined the French. In 1752, under the leadership of Charles de Langlade, a man of French and Ottawa ancestry, Ottawa warriors from Michilimackinac swept south to destroy an English trading post among the Miami at present-day Piqua, Ohio. Wasson, an Ojibwa war leader from Saginaw Bay, played a significant

FORTS AND OJIBWA VILLAGES, 1720–61

Lake of the Woods

Rainy Lake

Ft. St. Anne

Ft. Michipic

Ft. St. Pierre

Ft. Kaministikwia

Thunder Bay

Red River

Red Lake

Leech Lake

St. Louis River

LAKE SUPERIOR

Michipicoten Bay

Keweenaw Bay

Whitefish B

Crow Wing River

Ft. La Pointe

Chequamegon Bay

(Br. 1761)
Ft. Michilimacki

River

MINNESOTA

L'Arbre Croche

St. Croix River

WISCONSIN

Green Bay

Minnesota River

Ft. St. Pierre

Black River

Ft. La Baye
Ft. Edward
Augustus
(Br. 1761)

MICHIG

Ft. Beauharnois
Ft. La Jonquiere

Ft. Linctot

LAKE MICHIGAN

Mississippi

Milwaukee

Ft. Marin

IOWA

River

Waukegan

Chicago

Ft. St. Jos
(Br. 1761)

Ft. St. Phi

Ft. Ottawa

Ft. Pimitoui

River

Ft. Ouiat
(Br. 17

ILLINOIS

INDIA

Wabash

■	French fort/trading post
□	French trading post
⌐	British fort/trading post
⊠	British trading post
▲	Ojibwa villages

Ft. Vincenn

Ft. Chartes

(modern state and international boundaries)

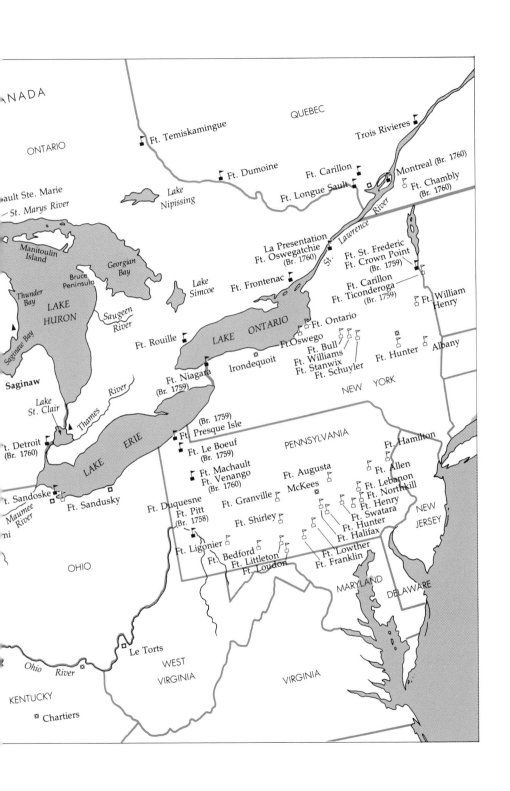

role in defeating the British general Edward Braddock in western Pennsylvania in 1755. This skirmish, which resulted in 900 British casualties, was one of the first major battles of the French and Indian War (1754–63).

Ojibwa from as far west as Chequamegon Bay fought alongside the French south of Lake Champlain, New York. Lake Superior Ojibwa were also present when the British defeated the French in Quebec in 1759. Montreal was forced to surrender the following year, ending France's rule in North America. In the Treaty of Paris in 1763, the agreement that concluded the war, France ceded its Canadian territory and all of its land east of the Mississippi River to Great Britain; the Louisiana Territory west of the Mississippi River went to Spain.

Although the British were ultimately victorious on the Pennsylvania front and in the conquest of Canada, Indian people maintained a strong allegiance to the French. Instead of trying to change Indian culture, the French had acquired an understanding of Indian customs. Many had married Ojibwa women and fulfilled their obligations to the tribe by providing for their Indian relatives.

French officials had also come to understand the significance of gifts in Indian society, where friends and allies regularly exchanged presents. To the Ojibwa, the greatness of a man was de-

In one of the first major battles of the French and Indian War (1754–63), the Indians helped the French defeat General Edward Braddock in western Pennsylvania in 1755. Wasson, an Ojibwa war leader from Saginaw Bay, played a significant role in this battle against British forces.

termined by what he gave away, not by what he could save for himself. In a society that believed in sharing, it was considered shameful to hoard one's goods.

On the other hand, the Indians regarded the annual gifts that they received in the name of the French king as a kind of rent. These gifts were considered a suitable exchange for the privilege of using land for forts in Indian country. If the English king was greater than the French king, they reasoned, English presents should be greater. The Indians were angered when the British actually gave them fewer presents and then behaved with arrogance rather than with respect for Indian leaders.

The first British military officials who arrived in Detroit, where the French command had surrendered in 1760, did not understand Indian values and their standards for proper behavior. They told the Great Lakes Indians that they should be ashamed for accepting gifts, which the British called "charity." The British also established strict new rules to regulate the fur trade, primarily prohibiting traders from granting the Indians credit. In addition, English settlers appeared intent on taking control of the entire region rather than merely trading their goods for furs.

Resentment among the Indians culminated in a widespread revolt, called Pontiac's Rebellion (1763–64). Pontiac, who encouraged various tribes to band together to drive the British from the Great Lakes region, was the leader of the Ottawa in Detroit. In April 1763, he began organizing a rebellion among the Potawatomi, Ottawa, and Huron villages there. The Seneca, the largest nation in the Iroquois Confederacy, and tribes in the Great Lakes and Ohio Valley, including Ottawa, Ojibwa, Mississauga, Miami, Shawnee, and Delaware Indians, also joined with Pontiac's forces.

The war began with a plot to seize 11 British forts between Pittsburgh and Green Bay. During late May and early June 1763, the Indians eliminated British detachments from nine forts, but the remaining two forts, at Pittsburgh and Detroit, survived long sieges. The most famous incident of Pontiac's Rebellion occurred at Fort Michilimackinac in present-day Michigan. Ojibwa warriors began playing a game of *baggataway*, or lacrosse, outside the fort with visiting Sauk Indians. Women and children cheered on the players, and the soldiers inside the fort were attracted by the noise. At a prearranged signal, an Ojibwa warrior shot a ball over the wall surrounding the fort. When the British soldiers opened the gate, the Indians rushed inside to retrieve the ball and then drew weapons and fired upon British soldiers. After capturing 70 soldiers, the Ojibwa easily took the fort.

Seizing Detroit and Pittsburgh proved to be more difficult for the Indians. During the summer of 1763, Pontiac's military force at Detroit consisted of as many as 870 warriors, including 250 Ottawas under Pontiac, 250 Ojibwas

A 19th-century engraving of the lacrosse game staged by Ojibwa and Sauk Indians at Fort Michilimackinac in 1763. In one of the most famous incidents of Pontiac's Rebellion, the Indians shot a ball over the wall of the garrison. Under the pretense of retrieving it, they were allowed through the gates. Once inside, they drew weapons and took the fort.

from Saginaw Bay under Wasson, 170 Mississauga Ojibwas from the Thames River under Sekahos, and 170 Potawatomis under Ninevois. In addition, Pontiac received the aid of 40 non-Christian Hurons and a few Menomi-nee from Green Bay. For a short time, he was joined by Mississauga from Toronto under Wabbomigot.

The British commanding officer, however, learned of Pontiac's plan to gain entrance to the fort on the pretense of holding a council. Pontiac's allies might well have been successful in storming the fort because the British garrison was guarded by only 120 soldiers. Nevertheless, Pontiac chose not to attack because Indian casualties would surely have been too high.

Before the fighting was suspended in the fall, Pontiac requested aid from the French. In October, the French commandant at Fort Chartres, in present-day Illinois, sent word to Pontiac that the French and British were at peace. The Indians were to stop fighting, for they would not receive aid from the French. Pontiac left Detroit at the end of the season of warfare in 1763, taking his followers to new village sites on the Maumee River west of present-day Toledo, Ohio. He soon moved on to sympathetic Indian communities on the Wabash River and eventually to southern Illinois.

Pontiac found it difficult to believe that the French were actually withdrawing from North America, as they had promised to do in the Treaty of Paris in 1763. Although the British had been victorious in Canada, Pontiac thought that the French in the province of Louisiana might be of some help. Not until Fort Chartres was relinquished to the British did Pontiac fully accept British rule.

Pontiac, however, still had supporters who would have continued warfare had he given the signal. Minevavana, known as Le Grand Saulteur, brought Ojibwa warriors from the Upper Peninsula of Michigan (the portion of the present-day state that borders Wisconsin) to a village on the Chicago River, where Potawatomi, Ojibwa, Ottawa, and Sauk warriors were living. Illinois Indians near Fort Chartres were also reluctant to accept British command. Sporadic attacks against the British continued to occur even after Pontiac's death in 1769.

Notwithstanding, the peace that had been established in 1764 during British councils at Detroit was relatively undisturbed. The Ojibwa at Michilimackinac and Sault Ste. Marie, as well as those in communities of the interior country, were eager to have traders return. To ensure a supply of European-made products, Indians accepted the British king as their new "Great Father." Experienced voyageurs and boatmen of French or French-Indian heritage began to work for British traders, as they had worked for the French. French families continued to live along the Detroit River and at Green Bay, as well as at Sault Ste. Marie and along the Straits of Mackinac.

Pontiac's Rebellion had demonstrated how widespread Indian resentment over British settlement had become. In the aftermath of the war, Sir William Johnson, the Indian superintendent in the northern district of British territory, held a conference at his headquarters near present-day Rome, New York. More than 3,000 Indians and representatives of the colonies attended the council. On November 5, 1768, representatives signed the Treaty of Fort Stanwix, fixing the Ohio River as the boundary line separating Indian country from territory for non-Indian settlement.

Lawless frontier settlers who refused to respect the boundary line caused 20 years of warfare in the Ohio Valley. Indians of all tribes tried to prevent the continued encroachment of the settlers, whom the Ojibwa called *Chemokoman*, or Big Knives. On the front line were the Shawnee, whose villages were closest to the Ohio River and Kentucky hunting grounds, but Ojibwa and Ottawa joined the war parties. Ojibwa from the Ontario peninsula and St. Clair River region often crossed Lake Erie in the fall to hunt in northern Ohio.

The warfare between Indians and Kentuckians in the Ohio Valley became more violent after the outbreak of the American Revolution (1775–83). For the most part, Indians on the Canadian side of Lake Ontario and Lake Erie were not affected by the Revolution. British traders and Indian hunters had a mutual interest in preserving hunting grounds, whereas the American colonists were more interested in gaining land for farms. Although the Revolution did not interrupt trade in the upper Great Lakes, the British Indian agents in Mackinac and Detroit continued to supply guns and ammunition needed for hunting.

At the beginning of the Revolution, both the British Indian agent in Detroit and the Americans in Pittsburgh vied for Indian allies. Wasson, the Ojibwa leader at Saginaw, attended American-sponsored councils in Pittsburgh in 1775, whereas Ojibwa and Ottawa delegations were present at British councils held in Detroit throughout the war.

Indians who supported the British lost homes and crops during raids by the American militia but never really suffered military defeat. At the end of the Revolution, they were outraged to learn that European diplomats had gathered in Paris without any Indian representation to discuss control over Indian land. The Treaty of Paris of 1783 greatly altered the boundary between Indian land and non-Indian territory as established by the Treaty of Fort Stanwix in 1768. The British agreed to withdraw from the country east of the Mississippi and south of the Great Lakes. Their surrender of this territory to the new American nation would greatly affect the settlement of the Ohio Valley.

British traders in Canada, however, held out hope for the formation of an Indian buffer state north of the Ohio River in order to continue the fur trade. The British tried in diplomatic cessions to block out land for Indian people to create an intermediary geographic area between the British and the Americans. For this reason, British garrisons remained in Detroit and Mackinac Island until another treaty was negotiated, requiring them to turn over the forts at Mackinac Island and Detroit to Americans in 1796. British traders did not entirely abandon this idea of an Indian buffer state until after the War of 1812.

Because settlers continued to encroach on Indian land following the American Revolution, the Ohio Valley

When the British commander at Fort Detroit discovered Pontiac's plan of attack, the Indian leader decided not to risk high casualties by storming the garrison. After a six-month siege, the Indian forces withdrew to the Maumee River.

TRIBAL DISTRIBUTION (ca. 1768)

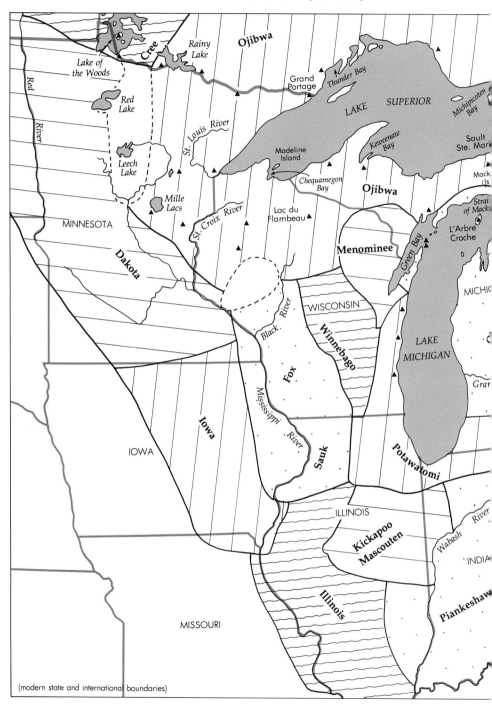

(modern state and international boundaries)

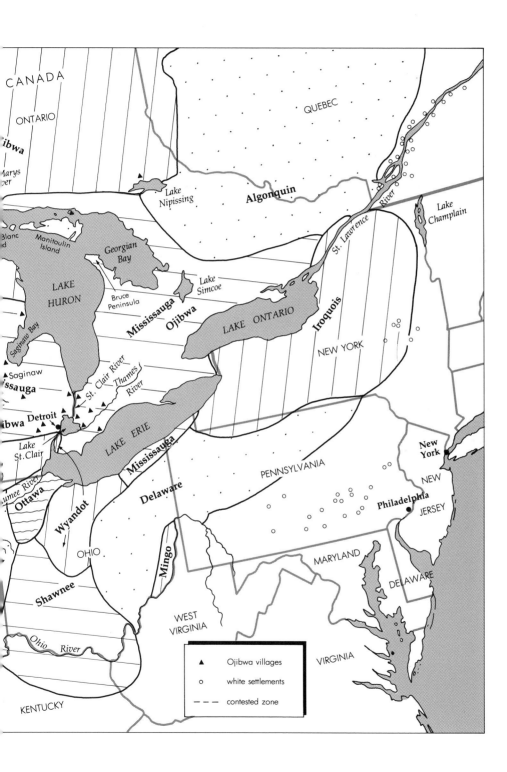

CANADA

ONTARIO

...ibwa

...Marys
...ver

Lake
Nipissing

Algonquin

QUEBEC

Lake
Champlain

St. Lawrence River

...Blanc

Manitoulin
Island

Georgian
Bay

LAKE
HURON

Bruce
Peninsula

Lake
Simcoe

LAKE ONTARIO

Iroquois

NEW YORK

Mississauga   Ojibwa

Saginaw Bay

Saginaw

...ssauga

St. Clair River

Thames
River

...ibwa Detroit

Lake
St.Clair

LAKE ERIE

Mississauga

New
York

NEW

...umee River

Ottawa

Mississauga

Delaware

PENNSYLVANIA

Philadelphia

JERSEY

Wyandot

OHIO

Mingo

MARYLAND

DELAWARE

Shawnee

WEST
VIRGINIA

VIRGINIA

Ohio   River

KENTUCKY

▲   Ojibwa villages

o   white settlements

- - -   contested zone

warfare continued. In 1787, frontiersman Daniel Boone arranged a peace council and an exchange of prisoners between military leaders of the Shawnee and settlers of present-day Kentucky, with plans for the Kentuckians to become trading partners with the Shawnee. However, renegade Kentuckians attacked a Shawnee town a few months later, and fighting resumed.

Ojibwa war parties from the Saginaw River valley were active along the Ohio River, plundering boats and taking captives. One of the best-known captives was a boy named John Tanner, who was captured on the south bank of the Ohio River in 1789 and taken to the Saginaw Bay area. He was later traded to an Ottawa family in northwestern Michigan. With them he moved to the Red River country and went on hunting expeditions into Manitoba. Living 30 years among the Ottawa and Ojibwa, he forgot the English language and adopted the Great Lakes Indian way of life. Tanner relearned English while acting as an official interpreter at Sault Ste. Marie in the 1830s. On Mackinac Island, he narrated his life story to Edwin James, an army doctor, who published the account.

During the final phase of the Ohio border wars, Indians turned back three U.S. Army expeditions launched from present-day Cincinnati in 1790 and 1791. The last was possibly the most humiliating defeat ever suffered by an American force. By that time, however, the allied Indian forces had all retreated to the Maumee River in northwest Ohio. Finally, in 1794, a reduced Indian army was overcome by specially trained troops led by General Anthony Wayne, who had additional help from the Kentucky militia. The site of the final battle was a cyclone-ravaged area called Fallen Timbers on the Maumee River west of Toledo, Ohio.

An engraving of Daniel Boone. In an attempt to stop the Ohio Valley warfare and to form a trade alliance between Indians and settlers, Daniel Boone arranged a peace council and an exchange of prisoners.

continued on page 65

KEEPING TRADITION ALIVE

For personal adornment, Ojibwa women traditionally decorated clothing with materials gathered from the land. They made beads by shaping or piercing bits of shell, bone, and stone. They also dyed and flattened the quill, or hollow shaft, of bird feathers and porcupine spines. By sewing or weaving these beads and quills onto animal hide, Ojibwa women created colorful geometric designs on a variety of items, including moccasins, medicine bags, and leggings.

All Ojibwa wore ornamented clothing, but the women alone were the artisans. As soon as a girl reached the age of seven or eight, her mother taught her the craft of beadwork. She learned how to make a pattern of holes in animal hide using a thorn or a split bone. Through these holes she could thread quills or sinew, on which beads were strung.

With the introduction of European trade goods in the early 17th century, young girls learned to work with new tools, such as steel needles and metal awls. Beadworkers discarded traditional raw materials for woven fabrics, cotton and linen thread, and ribbons. They also obtained colorful, mass-produced glass beads from either traders or missionaries, who wished to convert the Indians to Christianity. Because glass beads were easier to use, were more durable, and could be sewn into many elaborate patterns, women began to use fewer geometric patterns and adopted floral motifs.

After the late 19th century, when whites in the United States and Canada tried to assimilate Indians into their culture, the Ojibwa relinquished much of their traditional way of life and began to dress in non-Indian fashion, using very little beadwork to ornament their clothing. Their craft, however, did survive. A few women have learned the techniques once passed from mother to daughter, and beaded garments are still worn by Ojibwa who attend powwows and other events.

An Ojibwa moccasin decorated in both geometric and floral designs.

Intricate beadwork ornaments the tops and flaps of a pair of Ojibwa moccasins. Inspired by the floral patterns on white people's cloth, Indian women improvised their own designs.

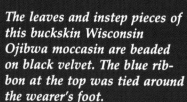

The leaves and instep pieces of this buckskin Wisconsin Ojibwa moccasin are beaded on black velvet. The blue ribbon at the top was tied around the wearer's foot.

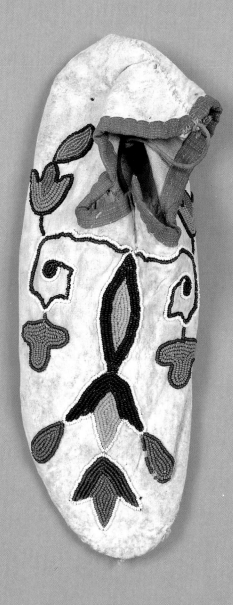
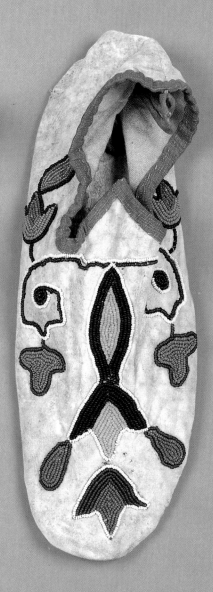

These Minnes___ ___e beaded in a
colorful flora___

This Ojibwa medicine bag from the Minnesota White Earth Reservation is made of cloth decorated in a beaded floral design. The baldric is a good specimen of Ojibwa bead weaving.

A beaded Ojibwa ceremony bag. By the mid-19th century, Indian bags were larger, primarily made of trade cloth, and more heavily beaded than were 18th-century bags.

A multicolored Ojibwa beaded haversack with tassels of red flannel.

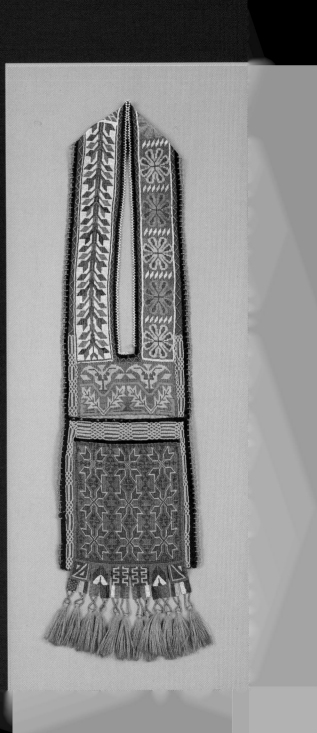

This Ojibwa red flannel bag from Canada sports multicolored glass beads arranged in diverse geometric designs on its outer side. Tassels made of woolen yarn skirt the beaded fringes. Small octagonal copper beads are arranged in a series of half loops about the bag's outer edge.

This oval-shaped Ojibwa beaded stole has a hole cut near the center to pull over one's head. Covered with floral patterned beadwork, the stole is edged with fringes consisting of short strands of glass beads ending in small copper bells.

An Ojibwa cloth-beaded skullcap made of triangular sections of red wool strouding, each one outlined in opaque white glass beads with floral designs in green and clear glass beads. On top is a fully beaded rectangular tassel in white, blue, and green. Inside are the remains of a paper lining through which the beads were sewn. This skullcap was part of a full costume made by a Michigan Ojibwa woman for her grandfather.

An Ojibwa beaded vest. The front is made of leather, with various designs in colored beads, while the back is made of

continued from page 56

During the summer of 1795, representatives of 13 Indian tribes involved in warfare over the Ohio River border gathered for a peace treaty in Greenville, Ohio. There were 46 Ojibwas, from as far as Sault Ste. Marie and the shores of Lake Superior, present at the Greenville treaty councils. Two leaders of the Ojibwa, Machipinashiwich and Massas, were among the principal speakers and often represented the Three Fires.

Under the terms of the treaty, they gave up the southern two-thirds of Ohio to American settlement. This was land that Americans had been demanding since the end of the American Revolution. Although American representatives had made three previous treaties with the Indians, in 1785, 1786, and 1789, concerning this same southern Ohio land, the agreements had been made without adequate tribal representation and were not officially recognized by the Indians.

In addition to land, the Greenville treaty gave the American government the right to build forts at 16 key geographic locations along the streams, on the islands, and at the portage points that were central to the Indians' communication network from the Ohio River to the Mississippi River. These areas included Mackinac Island, Chicago, and a six-mile stretch along the Detroit River. The treaty also stipulated that future Indian land sales could only be made to the United States.

By the end of the 18th century, non-Indians were pouring into the Northwest Territory along the Ohio River, and the governor of Indiana Territory was acquiring more and more land from the Indians, as far west as the Mississippi. The Ojibwa and other Great Lakes tribes became apprehensive of the United States. Some looked for a way to rid themselves of these persistent intruders.

Two Shawnee brothers mobilized resistance against non-Indian settlers. Tecumseh organized an Indian confederacy. His brother, Tenskwatawa, known as the Prophet, urged Indians to return to the old ways of their ancestors and to discard all things introduced by the white race. If they did this, the Great Spirit would deliver them from their dependence on the non-Indians.

Followers of the Prophet came to Lac Courte Oreilles in northern Wisconsin in 1808 and described his teachings to the Ojibwa. They then invited the Ojibwa to come to Detroit, where Tenskwatawa would explain to them personally the revelations of the Great Spirit. According to William W. Warren, the son of an Ojibwa woman and author of *History of the Ojibway People*, the Shawnee cult "spread like wild-fire throughout their entire country, and even reached the remotest northern hunters who had allied themselves with the Crees and Assiniboins." The Ojibwa who gathered near La Pointe threw away their medicine bags and performed ceremonies of the new religion both night and day.

At last this group decided to go see the Prophet. In 150 canoes, the new

Tenskwatawa, known as the Prophet, encouraged Indians to return to the old way of life and discard material goods introduced by non-Indians. His brother, Tecumseh, organized an Indian confederacy that opposed the presence of American settlers in Indian country.

converts traveled as far as Pictured Rocks, near Grand Island, before meeting up with Michel Cadotte, a trader from Lac Courte Oreilles. Cadotte was well respected among his neighbors. He convinced the Ojibwa that the Prophet was only interested in amassing an army to fight non-Indians. Most of the Ojibwa turned back. The few who ventured to Detroit came home disappointed and claimed that those who followed the Prophet were starving.

In 1811, anti-American hostility flared in present-day Ohio, Indiana, and Illinois. Even before the British and the Americans went to war, many followers of Tecumseh and Tenskwatawa opposed the presence of the Americans. The War of 1812, a conflict between American and British forces, led the British to cooperate with the militant Indians. Ojibwa people living in the eastern Great Lakes area participated in the fighting.

At the end of the war, the British regime in the upper Great Lakes region, which was principally a commercial enterprise controlled by Montreal traders, was replaced by the Americans. British presence in the Great Lakes area had only minimally affected Ojibwa culture. As late as 1814, few settlers had come to the area. The British traders, who came to make a profit, protected traditional culture, for it produced good hunters and trappers. The United States, on the other hand, was more interested in increasing non-Indian settlement throughout the Northwest; it was also determined to extend its authority over the Indians who lived in this newly acquired region. ▲

Lewis Cass, an American officer in the War of 1812, became gover-nor and superintendent of Indian affairs for Michigan Territory in 1813.

ENDURING "CIVILIZATION"

In the aftermath of the War of 1812, the American government slowly began to exert an influence over the Indians of the Great Lakes region. General Lewis Cass, who had led American forces against the British and Indians during the war, became governor of Michigan Territory in 1813, with headquarters in Detroit.

At that time, the non-Indian civilian population of the Detroit district consisted of about 2,000 French Canadians. Most of the British residents had moved across the Detroit River into Canada when British troops withdrew from Detroit in 1796. By contrast, the Indian population of the hinterland in the Lower Peninsula of Michigan was probably between 10,000 and 15,000. Closest to the post were the Potawatomi living in villages located within 40 miles of Detroit and extending across the peninsula to Lake Michigan. To the north were the Ojibwa of the St. Clair River and Saginaw Bay regions.

Unlike the Ojibwa west of Lake Superior, both the Potawatomi and Ojibwa living in Michigan's Lower Peninsula had been actively anti-American during the War of 1812. Though the United States had won the war, a British community with a fort and Indian allies still occupied the Canadian shore of the Detroit River opposite the American city of Detroit. Cass realized that Detroit, the frontier capital of Michigan Territory, was surrounded by enemies.

As governor and superintendent of Indian affairs for Michigan Territory, Cass arranged peace treaties with regional Indians, wresting land from those with whom he made peace. In 1817, he secured a major cession of territory in Ohio at the western end of Lake Erie. In 1819, he managed to force a land cession treaty on the Ojibwa of Saginaw Bay. Land closer to Detroit had already been sold by Ojibwa and Potawatomi in 1807, but the boundary had not been surveyed.

In the spring of 1820, Cass led the first American exploring expedition into the Ojibwa country of present-day northern Michigan, Wisconsin, and Minnesota. Heading northward along Lake Huron in three canoes, the Cass expedition covered 4,000 miles of waterways to Lake Superior and the Mississippi River before returning from Fort Dearborn (present-day Chicago) to Detroit on horseback in the fall.

Early in the trip, at Sault Ste. Marie, the governor encountered the Ojibwa, who still flew the British flag in defiance of American authority. Tension was dispelled by Oshawguscodaywayqua (Woman of the Green Prairie), or Susan, the Ojibwa wife of local British trader John Johnston; and Cass succeeded in negotiating a treaty permitting the establishment of an American garrison, Fort Brady, on the St. Marys River.

With the founding of the fort in 1822 and the return of Henry Rowe Schoolcraft, a mineralogist with the Cass expedition, the Americanization of the upper Great Lakes commenced. Schoolcraft, the federal government's official representative (known as an Indian agent) for Fort Brady, married John and Susan Johnston's daughter Jane. He

The Cass expedition leaves in the spring of 1820 for Ojibwa country in present-day northern Michigan, Wisconsin, and Minnesota. Before returning on horseback to Detroit in the fall, Lewis Cass covered 4,000 miles of waterways.

With the establishment of Fort Brady at Sault Ste. Marie, Michigan, in 1822 and the appointment of Henry Rowe Schoolcraft as Indian agent, the Americanization of the upper Great Lakes commenced.

also attained national recognition for his research and writing about Indian history, tradition, and language.

The initial treaties with the U.S. government and the presence of Schoolcraft and other Indian agents did not greatly alter the Ojibwa's way of life. However, as a consequence of a U.S. law passed in 1816 that prevented British merchants from conducting trade in American territory, trade arrangements changed.

Some Ojibwa and Ottawa hunters and trappers chose to continue working with British firms. They moved northwest of Lake Superior into Canadian hunting territory, where the Cree population had decreased severely because of an epidemic. When the heyday of the fur trade was over in the 1830s, many Ojibwa from the Sault Ste. Marie district remained in the Lake Winnipeg district of Canada, but a number of Ottawa returned to the L'Arbre Croche region in western Michigan.

Those Ojibwa who chose to trade with the Americans and the British traders who changed their allegiance dealt with a new and very powerful fur company. The trade law opened new markets for the American Fur Company, owned by John Jacob Astor. Until 1834, when Astor sold his holdings to a New York firm, his trading posts ranged the expanse of Ojibwa country, with headquarters on Mackinac Island, La Pointe, and at Fond du Lac.

During these years, the Ojibwa in American territory became extremely dependent on American traders. For example, Indians in the Keweenaw region and those living as far west as Fond du Lac fished the bays with nets and spears; but during the winter the Indians were often reduced to procuring provisions from traders because the territory had been depleted of bears, deer, and other large game.

As settlers moved into present-day Wisconsin and Minnesota, the U.S. government began to take precautionary measures to protect the farmers and regulate trade. Forts were built at Green Bay, Prairie du Chien, and at the junction of the Minnesota and Mississippi rivers. Then the Bureau of Indian Affairs (BIA), a federal agency in charge of trade and Indian relations, invited nearby tribes to a grand council at Prairie du Chien in August 1825. The principal objective was to end the long-standing Sioux-Ojibwa conflict. The

American Fur Company buildings at Fond du Lac, at the western end of Lake Superior. As a consequence of a U.S. law passed in 1816 preventing British merchants from conducting trade in American territory, new markets were opened for John Jacob Astor and his American Fur Company. The Ojibwa became increasingly dependent on these American traders.

two nations had been at war since 1736, when the Sioux turned against the Ojibwa's French allies. More than 1,000 leaders representing the Sioux, Ojibwa, Sauk, Fox, Menominee, Iowa, Winnebago, and the intermixed Ottawa, Ojibwa, and Potawatomi living on the Illinois River came to Fort Crawford, the military post guarding Prairie du Chien at the mouth of the Wisconsin River.

In preparation for the grand council, Henry Rowe Schoolcraft assembled 150 Ojibwas and 60 soldiers and musicians from the Mackinac district. This delegation traveled by canoe through Green Bay and the Fox–Wisconsin River route, completing the trip to Prairie du Chien in 19 days. From Fort Snelling at present-day Minneapolis–St. Paul, Indian agent Lawrence Taliaferro descended the Mississippi River with 365 Ojibwa and Sioux Indians. Before completing the final stretch, the entire fleet of canoes stopped to put on festive attire, then arrived with flags flying, guns firing, and drums beating.

In the treaty drawn up at Prairie du Chien in 1825, the first article announced proclaimed peace between the Sioux and the Ojibwa, and a later provision described a boundary between the territories of the two tribes. The boundary nearly bisected present-day Minnesota, running southeast into what is now Wisconsin. The tribes could cross it only if they were on peaceful missions.

Because several bands of Ojibwa did not attend the 1825 council at Prairie du Chien, a follow-up council took place the next year at Fond du Lac, an Ojibwa town and American Fur Company post near the mouth of the St. Louis River outside of present-day Duluth. The Treaty of Fond du Lac in 1826 marked an important milestone in the history of American government relations with Indian people in several ways.

Thomas L. McKenney, the first commissioner of Indian affairs, came all the way from Washington, D.C., to attend the council. For his first treaty on the American frontier, among such a prestigious gathering of Indians, McKenney brought along artist James O. Lewis, who sketched the treaty site and drew portraits of a number of Ojibwa who came from the area between Sault Ste. Marie and Rainy River, on the northern border of present-day Minnesota.

Following the custom for all open-air Indian councils, the Ojibwa had built a large structure made of posts and cross poles and covered with leafy branches to protect the assembly from the August sun. Thomas McKenney and Lewis Cass were the official treaty commissioners. In addition to Indians and government representatives, military personnel and traders were also present.

The other important government representative at Fond du Lac in 1826 was Henry Rowe Schoolcraft. On this occasion, Schoolcraft brought a substantial delegation of Sault Ste. Marie leaders, including his mother-in-law, Susan Johnston, who had considerable status as daughter of the famous La Pointe leader Waubojig (White Fisher).

*A drawing made by James O. Lewis of the treaty council held at Prairie du Chien in 1825.
More than 1,000 leaders representing Sioux, Ojibwa, Sauk, Fox, Menominee, Iowa, Winne-
bago, and other tribes gathered to meet Indian agents and commissioners representing the
United States government.*

She was the subject of one of the Lewis portraits, though the portrait is not very flattering.

The main business of the treaty, gaining the assent of more Ojibwa to the Treaty of Prairie du Chien, was easily accomplished. The Indian leaders also "disclaimed connection with any foreign power," obviously a reference to their recent alliance with the British. They further agreed to come to Green Bay in 1827 to establish boundaries with the Menominee and the Winnebago. Other articles of the treaty focused at-

tention on Sault Ste. Marie, calling for a $2,000 annual payment, or annuity. Also, a sum of $1,000 a year was set aside for the construction of a school on the St. Marys River, the first educational institution for the Ojibwa in Michigan Territory.

Neither the Treaty of Prairie du Chien nor the Treaty of Fond du Lac actually stopped the fighting between the Ojibwa and the Sioux. Although most of the Ojibwa still living around the Great Lakes had stopped fighting with the Sioux by the 1830s, Ojibwa living along the Mississippi, at Leech Lake, and at Red Lake continued the feud until the 1850s. The Minnesota Sioux fled or were confined to a reservation in Nebraska after rising up against non-Indians in Minnesota in 1862.

The non-Indian population increased dramatically in the 1830s in present-day southern Michigan. Following the opening of the Erie Canal in 1825 and the beginning of steamship navigation on the Great Lakes, new residents poured into Detroit from eastern states and Europe. By 1834, more than 86,000 people lived in the territory east of Lake Michigan. The number doubled by 1837, when Michigan became a state.

The government was eager to wrest control of the land north of the Grand River from the Ottawa and Ojibwa. Land in the southwest corner of Michigan, south of Grand River, had already been ceded at a treaty council at Chicago in 1821. In 1836, the Ottawa and Ojibwa of what is now western Michigan and the eastern end of the Upper Peninsula were drawn into a major land cession, partially through their own actions.

Indian fishermen on the north shore of Lake Michigan wanted government protection for their fishing grounds, which were being threatened by an American Fur Company takeover. The Ottawa people of L'Arbre Croche and Little Traverse Bay learned that new federal legislation in 1835 might call for the cancellation of blacksmith services to the Indians. The Ojibwa were willing

Susan Johnston, or Oshawguscodaywayqua, enjoyed considerable status as daughter of La Pointe leader Waubojig. Along with a delegation from Sault Ste. Marie, she accompanied Schoolcraft to the treaty site at Fond du Lac in 1826, where her portrait was drawn by Lewis. (From McKenny, Tour to the Lakes.)

to make concessions in order to stop this legislation, for they had come to count on the blacksmith to repair guns and traps and to make fishing spears and ice cutters.

After independent Indian delegations from Michigan went to Washington in the fall of 1835, Henry Rowe Schoolcraft organized a group of Ottawa and Ojibwa to participate in official negotiations. He included in the treaty delegation his wife's Ojibwa uncle and cousin as Upper Peninsula rep-

LAND CESSIONS (1783–1873)

(modern state and international boundaries)

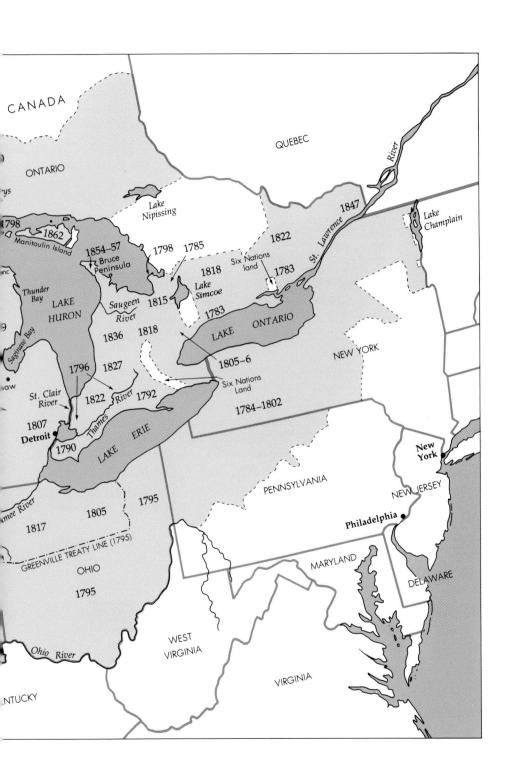

resentatives. Schoolcraft was eager to gain a cession of land in the Upper Peninsula of Michigan, already known for its copper resources. On his tour with Governor Cass in 1820, he had seen the famous Ontonagon boulder, which contained more than 20 cubic feet of solid copper and weighed 6,000 pounds.

The treaty assured the Indians the services of three blacksmiths; the right to hunt and fish on the land they were "selling"; reservations located at their special fishing grounds; and an annual supply of tobacco, salt, and barrels for packing fish. The government also provided gifts of between $100 and $500 to each of the 147 leaders of the bands represented and a $300,000 payment to the American Fur Company for debts the company claimed were owed by these Indian groups. The treaty designated an additional $150,000 for half bloods, relatives of the Indians, many of whom were also related to the traders.

In 1830, both the British and American officials tried to move Indian people into areas away from the new non-Indian settlements. At first, U.S. officials considered establishing a northern Indian territory on the upper Mississippi River for Great Lakes Indians. But in 1837 that land, in present-day Minnesota and Wisconsin, was ceded to the federal government and was therefore no longer available as a regional Indian homeland. The Ottawa and Ojibwa bands involved in the March 28, 1836 treaty were encouraged to relocate, or "remove," to Missouri, but they re-

fused to consider the possibility. By 1841, the government had given up any thought of moving the western Michigan Ojibwa and Ottawa.

Beginning in May 1836 and continuing through 1837, the Ojibwa of Saginaw, Swan Creek, and Black River in lower eastern Michigan engaged in several treaty negotiations with the federal government. Although they gave up rights to reservations created previously in eastern Michigan, only about 60 Swan Creek Ojibwas actually moved west of the Mississippi.

In Canada, the British Indian Department announced a "civilization" program in 1830. The objective of this program was to place the Ojibwa on reserved areas where they would settle down and learn to live by farming rather than by fishing, hunting, and gathering berries. The most widely publicized example of this new program was Coldwater Reserve, located at the north end of Lake Simcoe. The reserve existed for only six years. The bands at Coldwater sold their reserve in 1836 and dispersed to other places in Southern Ontario. Other Canadian reserves established in the 1830s were located at Rice Lake, Mud Lake, and Lake Scugog, where the Mississauga purchased their own land with annuity money from previous land sales.

The lieutenant governor of Canada, Sir Francis Bond Head, added a removal plan to the "civilization" program in 1836, but the project turned out to be as unsuccessful for the British as it was for the Americans. Bond Head thought that Indian people would be better off if they lived as they preferred, but he believed that they needed to be away from the non-Indian settlements where whiskey was sold. He decided to go to Manitoulin Island to be present for the annual distribution of gifts to an estimated 7,000 Indians from the upper Great Lakes.

The British government had distributed gifts to Indian allies each year since the end of the War of 1812 in appreciation of Indian services during the war. Many of the visitors came from American territory west of Lake Michigan and Lake Superior for the annual gathering, which included games, races, ceremonies, and dancing.

While he was at Manitoulin Island in August 1836, Bond Head secured questionable agreement to two propositions. He proposed that the Ojibwa living around the Saugeen River, on the southeast shore of Lake Huron, cede the southern part of their territory and move out onto the Bruce Peninsula. At the same time, he proposed that the assembled Indians give the Manitoulin Islands to the government to be administered as a reserve for all Indian people. He actually hoped that the Saugeen Indians would remove to Manitoulin Island along with several thousand Indians from other parts of Canada and the United States.

A number of Indian leaders signed the agreement, some only because they did not want to offend the chief executive of Canada. Later, the Ojibwa of the Saugeen district vigorously protested

the opening of their best lands to settlement and finally received compensation. The rocky islands of the Manitoulin chain, where fishing was the principal source of livelihood, had little land suitable for agriculture.

Missionaries in Canada and the United States were enthusiastic promoters of "civilization" programs. They believed that conversion to Christianity would be made easier if Indian people were assembled in one place. However, the Ojibwa had as yet no real reason to modify their way of life. Copper miners and lumbermen, on the other hand, presented a challenge. Soon after they had poured into the rich Ojibwa homeland, they were demanding the removal of the Indians to another territory.

In the 1840s, when copper mining boomed on the south shore of Lake Superior in present-day Wisconsin and Minnesota, the U.S. government allowed Ojibwa to remain in the ceded region. Farmers were not interested in the land there, for the winters were harsh and the growing season was short. However, the BIA recommended the removal of the Ojibwa to west of the Mississippi, where they could farm and live in permanent houses.

The Ojibwa would not agree to such an arrangement and sent several spokesmen to Washington in 1849 to obtain ownership of the land they were living on, as well as their maple sugar, and rice lakes. The Ojibwa insisted that they had never given up their land and had only made allowances for the copper to be mined. Removal was abandoned, and the government began to plan consolidating the Ojibwa on reservations in northern Minnesota. Treaties in 1863 and 1867 called for two large reservations at Leech Lake and White Earth. Later, in 1889, another reservation was established at Red Lake.

By 1850, U.S. officials decided that they needed to make permanent living arrangements for several thousand Ojibwa and Ottawa who resided in Michigan and Wisconsin. Lumber and mining companies wanted to begin large-scale operations, and farm communities had already begun to spread across the state. In addition, owing to provisions of a new state constitution in 1850, Indian men could now vote in Michigan. They represented a significant voting block in the unsettled northern part of the state. Some even held local offices.

Beginning in 1854, the U.S. government launched a second stage in the reservation program—allotting individual Indian families plots within reserved areas. Treaties were made with the Ojibwa on the headwaters of the Mississippi River in Minnesota, the Ojibwa of Lake Superior, and various bands in the Upper and Lower peninsulas of Michigan. During July 1855, a final treaty conference took place at Detroit for representatives of all the Ojibwa and Ottawa in the Michigan Lower Peninsula as well as the Sault Ste. Marie district of the Upper Peninsula. A stated objective of the treaties

was to provide permanent homes for these Indians.

The Indian leaders had a number of complaints to make about payments owed to them by the government. Settlers had taken game that the Indians had dressed and left hanging in the woods during hunting season. The schools financed by the government actually educated only the traders' children rather than the children of Indian families. In addition, the Sault Ste. Marie delegation that came to Detroit was still irate about the construction of a shipping canal that had destroyed their village and fishing sites, which were guaranteed to them by treaties signed in 1820 and 1836. The residents of the Ojibwa village had awakened one morning in June 1853 to find 400 workmen on their land. Most families fled to the south side of town after the workmen began constructing the canal. The first vessels loaded with iron ore passed through the locks in June 1855, before the aggrieved members of the Sault Ste. Marie band left for the council in Detroit.

At the end of spirited discussions about land, education, and payments owed to the Ojibwa, the assembled chiefs and headmen signed treaties on July 31 for the northwestern Michigan "Ottawas and Chippewas" and on August 2 for the Saginaw, Swan Creek, and Black River bands. A separate treaty, signed August 2 with the Sault Ste. Marie band, giving up their "permanent reserve," has been declared

Spearing Muskrat in Winter, *by Eastman. In the late 19th century, many Ojibwa continued to gather wild rice and to hunt and fish. However, because reservation lands lacked the natural resources necessary to support their population, the Ojibwa people began to adapt to a new way of life.*

fraudulent by the Indians. According to the two principal 1855 treaties, the government would provide individual farms with farming equipment and each farm family with carpentry tools. The federal land office would set aside blocks of land from which the members of each band could select acreage; the plots would be proportionate to the size of each family. The best land had already been acquired by the Sault Ste. Marie Canal Land Company as payment for building the canal.

The government never did carry out this plan to provide permanent homes for the Ojibwa and Ottawa by allotting land to each family. Real estate speculators, lumber firms, railroad companies, politicians, and settlers, sometimes working with Indian agents and federal land offices, interfered with the allotment process. When the General Allotment Act was passed in 1887, calling for the allotment of reservations, almost 90 percent of the land promised to Ojibwa and Ottawa families in the upper Great Lakes region had already passed into non-Indian possession.

On the reservations, the Ojibwa had to adapt to new circumstances. Although they wished to continue a traditional way of life, based on fishing and gathering wild rice, the reduced land lacked the natural resources essential to support their population. Furthermore, the BIA sought to destroy the Ojibwa's traditional culture and lifestyle and to force the Indians into cultivating the soil. Because of the government's efforts, in the next 50 years many Ojibwa would abandon their ancient ways forever. ▲

Hole-in-the-Day (the Younger) played a principal role in concluding the 1867 treaty that called for the creation of White Earth Reservation in Minnesota. He himself never occupied the reservation because he was shot and killed by an assassin while riding in his horse and buggy.

LOSING
GROUND

In the mid-19th century, after an influx of miners, lumberjacks, and settlers began to displace the Great Lakes Indians from their homeland, the U.S. government negotiated treaties with the Indians and set aside a number of reservations in Wisconsin, Michigan, and Minnesota. For the Ojibwa in Wisconsin, the government created reservations at Lac Courte Oreilles, Lac du Flambeau, Bad River, and Red Cliff, as well as on tracts of land for the St. Croix and Mole Lake bands. In the western Upper Peninsula of Michigan, the L'Anse and Lac Vieux de Sert bands received 90 square miles at the head of Keweenaw Bay. In northern Minnesota, the Fond du Lac and Grand Portage reservations were established, and a tract of land at Nett Lake was reserved for the Bois Forte band. Reservations were also established at Leech Lake, Sandy Lake, and other places on the headwaters of the Mississippi River in Minnesota.

In creating these reservations, the government not only sought to concentrate the Indians in a much smaller region but also hoped to "civilize" them. The BIA encouraged the Indians to live in permanent housing, to farm the land, and to send their children to reservation schools. Although the Ojibwa who lived in isolated villages managed to hold on to more of their traditional ways, many who settled on reservations eventually adopted a non-Indian way of life. At some of these reservations, the Ojibwa lived in cabins, dressed in non-Indian clothing, attended Christian church services, and sent their children to reservation schools, which taught the English language and gave lectures on patriotism.

Few Ojibwa were able to support themselves on the reservations by fishing, hunting, and foraging, although these endeavors supplemented their livelihood. Economic adjustment occurred because the reservations lacked

An Indian cemetery and church at Grand Portage Reservation in Minnesota in 1885. Living under the close scrutiny of government officials who controlled annuity payments and discouraged Indian traditions, many reservation Ojibwa began dressing in non-Indian clothing and attending Christian church services.

the resources needed to support the Ojibwa's traditional way of life and because new industries outside the reservations provided employment opportunities. The men living at Bad River and Red Cliff in Wisconsin worked in mills and in cooper, blacksmith, and carpentry shops. Some found jobs in the lumber industry, with mining companies, or on the railroads.

The Ojibwa also relied on annuity payments until the treaty terms ended. Congress continued to support reservation schools, blacksmiths, and farm-

ers even after appropriations set by the treaty had expired. The BIA, however, believed that the Ojibwa could become self-sufficient by learning to farm. Thus, it began to advocate a further concentration of the Indians on fewer reservations so that government staff could be reduced.

White Earth Reservation in Minnesota was created by treaty in 1867 for Ojibwa living at Mille Lacs and at five small reservations that had been established in 1855 along the upper region of the Mississippi River. A big square tract of land, 36 miles long on each side, in the northwestern part of Minnesota appeared to be an ideal new homeland. Small lakes and streams covered the land. Pine forests covered the eastern third of the reservation, whereas the western side boasted rich prairie soil. In the midsection grew mixed hardwoods.

The government tried, unsuccessfully, to force all of the Ojibwa in Minnesota to move to this location and encouraged them to farm there. To help the Ojibwa get started at White Earth, the 1867 treaty promised to provide them with farm implements, livestock, grain mills, blacksmiths, schools, and a doctor. In addition, the treaty specified that annuities would be distributed each year for clothing and provisions.

Hole-in-the-Day (the Younger), who lived at Gull Lake, played a principal

Indians receiving annuity payments at La Pointe, Wisconsin, around 1869. The Ojibwa depended on annuities from the government as well as employment opportunities outside the reservations because the limited tracts of land on which they lived lacked the natural resources to support their traditional way of life.

OJIBWA RESERVATIONS AND RESERVES TODAY

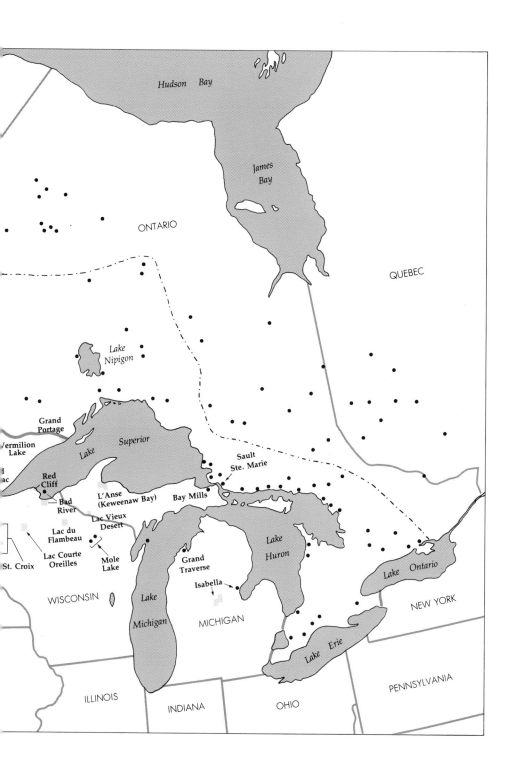

role in concluding the 1867 treaty as chief representative for all the bands involved. For his cooperation in making the treaty, Hole-in-the-Day received grants of money and a title for land at his farm bordering the Mississippi River. However, he never actually reached White Earth. He was fatally shot in October 1868 as he was riding in his buggy. It is believed that he was murdered because he did not consult leaders at Leech Lake before ceding land belonging to the Pillager bands in the 1867 treaty. His murder may also have been related to his blocking French Canadian traders from getting land at White Earth.

The first Ojibwa to relocate to White Earth arrived on June 14, 1868, from Gull Lake and Crow Wing River, west of the present-day town of Brainerd, Minnesota. However, little preparation had been made for these new prospective farmers, and many of them returned home for several years. The situation improved notably after an energetic agent arrived at the reservation in 1872. He promptly persuaded Congress to pass appropriation bills to finance some of the treaty provisions.

The reservation at first had only a few hundred permanent residents rather than the two to four thousand expected. When the population did begin to grow, with the arrival of Ojibwa outside the group of "Mississippi bands" for whom the reservation was originally created, dissension developed. Among the newcomers were a group of Pillagers, who had moved north from ceded land on the Otter Tail River, and some Pembina Ojibwa who had given up the lands on the Red River granted to them in an 1863 treaty.

A greater state of crisis developed at White Earth when settlers and lumber barons set their sights on the reservation lands. By 1886, the Ojibwa faced the prospect of losing much of their reservation. Timber companies wanted the pinelands on the eastern edge, and a new wave of European immigrants in the Red River valley demanded the farmland on the western side of the reservation where a railroad line was soon to be built. Thus, both settlers and lumbermen favored plans being made by Congress to divide up all Indian reservations by first allotting land for individual Indian farms, then selling the balance to non-Indians.

The original general allotment plan for Indian reservations was proposed by idealistic religious leaders living in the eastern part of the United States. These reformers believed that Indians should become farmers and live the "proper" American way of life. BIA officials, too, disapproved of the Indian customs of cooperative hunting, fishing, and rice gathering, calling this community-oriented way of life backward. Unfortunately for the Indians, the General Allotment Act that was passed by Congress in 1887 allowed land developers and other investors to acquire parts of the reservations.

White Earth was large enough to block out about 5,000 farms of 160 acres, the amount of land the General Allotment Act granted to each head of a household. Ojibwa residents realized that with a growing population some of this land should be saved for future generations. However, under the prospective allotment plan, any land not distributed to the present population of the reservation would be declared surplus and offered for sale to non-Indians. Thus, the Ojibwa opposed government efforts to divide up their land, hoping to keep it from falling into the hands of whites.

In 1886, the most outspoken opponents of the allotment plan at White Earth came from prominent members of the Beaulieu family, educated merchants and successful farmers who were descendants of a La Pointe trader. Augustus Beaulieu and his brothers started a newspaper in March 1886 to present their political views and, in particular, to explain their opposition to allotment. Because they had not secured permission from the federal agent at White Earth to publish a newspaper, the agent immediately closed the offices and confiscated the presses. The Beaulieus took the matter to a federal court in St. Paul, Minnesota, which agreed that the agent's actions had violated the freedom of the press. When the *Progress*

White Earth Reservation during a celebration on June 14, 1910. In 1909 an investigation revealed that 80 percent of the land at White Earth no longer belonged to Ojibwa residents but to banks, real estate developers, and timber companies. Many Indians were homeless squatters on their own reservation.

Girls' washroom at White Earth Mission School, which was founded in 1889. Ojibwa children not only learned non-Indian ways in school but were also forced to do the cleaning, cooking, sewing, and outdoor chores.

(later renamed the *Tomahawk*) resumed publication the following October, it was the only Indian newspaper being published outside of Indian Territory (present-day Oklahoma).

In spite of opposition on the reservation, Congress enacted allotment legislation for White Earth and other reservations, with the exception of Red Lake. In councils at the reservations, the government commissioners, aided by trusted clergymen and missionaries, finally persuaded most Ojibwa leaders to agree to the government plan. The Ojibwa were convinced that their families would all be very rich if they let the government sell "surplus" reservation land and timberland. The money would be placed in a special fund, drawing interest for 50 years, and then be distributed. In the meantime, the Ojibwa would receive annual interest payments that would increase each year as the fund grew.

Although the government again tried to consolidate all of the Ojibwa of Minnesota on White Earth Reservation, federal legislation allowed some Ojibwa to receive allotments on their old reservations. The Mille Lacs people, for example, demanded special treatment. They reminded the government that they had thwarted Hole-in-the-Day's plans for attacking forts and white settlers at the time of the Sioux Uprising in 1862. Their reservation still exists, though many people living at Mille Lacs agreed to move to a corner of White Earth in 1902.

Allotment legislation and other government measures for managing White Earth generally changed the reservation for the worse. An investigation in 1909 revealed that 80 percent of the land no longer belonged to the Ojibwa residents. Bankers and real estate developers had acquired most of the individual Indian farms, often by rapidly foreclosing on fraudulent mortgages or by using liquor to get Indians' signatures on land-sale papers. The timber companies made great profits by acquiring land and providing lumber for new towns and railroads. As a result of all this profiteering, many Ojibwa became homeless squatters on their own reservation.

By the early 20th century, White Earth presented a disturbing picture. Families were disheartened because their children were beaten at school if they spoke Ojibwa. Schools taught the "white" way of life and forced the students to do the school's cleaning, cooking, sewing, and farm chores. Health conditions were equally disturbing. Tuberculosis infected more than 60 percent of the population. One-third of the people suffered trachoma, an eye disease that causes blindness when left untreated. An estimated 20 percent of the population had contracted syphilis. To complicate matters further, saloons in the towns along the railroad on the western side of White Earth sold liquor illegally to the Indians.

The people at White Earth who considered themselves to be of all-Indian ancestry (full-bloods) attributed their misfortunes to the more economically successful members of the reservation whom they called the "mixed-bloods." By 1900, most Ojibwa had non-Indian lineages to varying degrees, but these two factions of Ojibwa were culturally very different.

The mixed-bloods lived in the town, or agency headquarters, of White Earth. They owned stores, published the newspaper, and earned money as government farmers and interpreters. They generally supported the Roman Catholic church.

The leading full-bloods lived around Pine Point, at the southeastern corner of the reservation, 20 miles from the agency. They continued the practices of the Midewiwin society or joined the Episcopal church. They also were more dependent on traditional economic pursuits, following the annual round of sugar making, hunting, fishing, ricing, and storing crops harvested from small gardens. They exchanged tanned leather and baskets at the store for cloth and nails; the mixed-bloods were more likely to use cash to purchase these items.

Open controversy between the two factions developed in 1911, when the full-bloods sent a petition to the BIA asking the government to delete the names of 86 mixed-bloods, including prominent leaders, from the list, or official roll, of Ojibwa at White Earth. The full-bloods maintained that the mixed-bloods were so "near white" that they should leave the reservation and go to live among white people. Charles T. Wright, the leader of the full-bloods and son of the venerated leader Wabanaquot (White Cloud), wanted government recognition as the new chief at White Earth. He succeeded in having the 86 mixed-bloods removed from the tribal roll.

Leaders of these mixed-bloods and representatives from all of the other Ojibwa reservations in Minnesota except Red Lake met in a general council at Leech Lake Reservation in 1913. The Pine Point contingent at White Earth reacted by organizing the full-blood faction, which sent a rival delegation to a general council meeting held at Bemidji in 1916. There a BIA inspector made the two delegations choose a single delegation with representatives from both groups.

The government wanted to end the influence of hereditary chiefs and traditional customs, which were considered to be evidence of paganism and "uncivilized" tribal ways. The mixed-bloods, also called progressives, appeared to be living in the "civilized" manner advocated by the government. Consequently, federal policy favored the general council, and the BIA reinstated the mixed-bloods to the tribal rolls in 1916. Although rivalry between traditionalists and progressives occurred on all Indian reservations, the struggle between these opposing factions at White Earth has been especially strong and enduring.

Leech Lake has a background quite different from that of the government-created White Earth Reservation. The Ojibwa settlements at Leech Lake are comparatively old, for the land was taken from the Sioux in the mid-18th century. Three separate clusters of Ojibwa communities gathered at Leech Lake, Cass Lake, and Lake Winnibigoshish. In an 1855 treaty, they were assigned separate reservations, but these were combined and their boundaries were changed during the next 20 years. Together they were known as the Pillagers.

Like other Ojibwa, the Pillagers accumulated grievances against the federal government after they began making treaties and ceding most of their land. They found that annual payments of supplies and money were not distributed according to treaty provisions. Furthermore, government representatives had promised large sums of money to these Ojibwa, to be raised from the sale of "surplus" land on the

Leech Lake Indian Agency around 1890. The Ojibwa at Leech Lake, Minnesota, had a special grievance with the government: More than 40,000 acres of rice fields were ruined when the U.S. Army Corps of Engineers built dams on the reservation in the 1880s.

reservations. Some land was distributed to other Ojibwa from Wisconsin or Michigan, but the Indians at Leech Lake received very little of the money. Some of it was used to send U.S. congressional commissions to Minnesota to inquire about the complaints.

At Leech Lake, however, the Pillager band had a special grievance—the loss of valuable rice fields. More than 40,000 acres of swamp were flooded when the U.S. Army Corps of Engineers built dams on the reservation in the 1880s. Reservation leaders considered the government's payment for this damage grossly inadequate.

One other source of aggravation at Leech Lake was the law enforcement system. Because officers received fees for every arrest they made, Ojibwa men were arrested at regular intervals by deputy marshals and taken to St. Paul or Duluth for trial. They were usually charged with selling liquor illegally or with witnessing such a sale. Frequently the arresting officer was involved in supplying the liquor leading to the arrest.

One Ojibwa leader at Leech Lake finally refused to submit to such treatment. His resistance led to the last battle involving Indian people and the U.S. Army in the eastern United States. Bugonegijig, leader of about 200 Ojibwas living on Bear Island, next to Sugar Point, was arrested in April 1895 on a liquor charge. No witness was produced, and he was set free. He had just

Bugonegijig (left) and two members of his tribe on Bear Island in 1897. The Ojibwa leader's resistance to an unjust law enforcement system at Leech Lake Reservation led to the last battle between Indian people and the U.S. Army.

recently been taken to Duluth as a witness and, not having funds to travel, had to walk a hundred miles back to the reservation. He was still very irritated when he received his next subpoena. He ignored it and was arrested. Then, after a dozen of his supporters released him from custody, he was sought for further arrest.

Because Bugonegijig and his closest followers continued to defy the government, plans were made to seize the chief when everyone came to the agency for annuity distribution on September 15, 1898. Although a deputy marshal successfully made the arrest, 50 men joined in releasing Bugonegijig and taking him to his home on Sugar Point. In response, the U.S. marshal in St. Paul requested military assistance from the War Department to serve warrants for the arrest of Bugonegijig and 21 other members of the Bear Island band. Close to 500 troops and a brigadier general had camped near the Indian agency by early October.

On the morning of October 5, two steamboats, one towing a bargeload of soldiers, set off across Leech Lake for Sugar Point. The military force marched around the point but saw only elderly men and women. Unfortunately, when the soldiers stacked their firearms for lunch, one of their guns accidentally discharged. Two signal shots immediately brought volleys of fire from Indians hidden in the surrounding woods. The officer commanding the military detachment and five others lost their life during the exchange of fire that

afternoon, but the Bear Islanders suffered no casualties.

On October 7, the American force returned to the mainland, expecting a larger campaign. More than a thousand troops arrived at Leech Lake by railroad. The general ordered detachments to guard the two dams on the Leech Lake Reservation, with additional units protecting the railroad stations in the vicinity. However, further military action was prevented when the commissioner of Indian affairs arrived from Washington to make immediate arrangements for peace. He secured a well-liked Catholic priest from the White Earth Reservation to serve as mediator. A canoeload of presents, including pork, flour, sugar, and the all-important gift of tobacco, set the stage for negotiations.

In council, the Leech Lake orators recounted to the commissioner the hardships and injustices they had experienced since non-Indians had come to their land. They also issued a formal statement expressing regret for the soldiers' lives lost at Sugar Point. The priest gradually persuaded 12 Bear Islanders to submit to arrest and accompanied the group to court in Duluth. For resisting arrest, the men were fined and sentenced to jail for periods up to 10 months.

Meanwhile, Bugonegijig was still at liberty, and the commissioner of Indian affairs felt that it was unjust for the co-operative Ojibwa to suffer stiff sentences while other offenders remained free. Because they had shown some re-

After 6 soldiers lost their life on Bear Island during a search for Bugonegijig, more than 1,000 troops were dispatched to Leech Lake by railroad on June 7, 1898. The commissioner of Indian affairs arrived in time to prevent further military action, and peace was restored.

gard for the law, he urged clemency. In January 1899, President William McKinley issued pardons to all of those charged in the Leech Lake incidents. Bugonegijig, on the other hand, remained a hero to his people. A new school set in the forest on the Leech Lake Reservation still carries his name.

Unlike White Earth and Leech Lake, where the government allotted separate plots of land to individual families, Red Lake Reservation remained a communal possession belonging to the entire tribe. Although they ceded more than 3,000 square miles of forest and swampland to the United States in 19th-century treaties, the Ojibwa at Red Lake Reservation kept the land surrounding the lake and thwarted all government efforts to divide their remaining land into privately owned parcels. Even to-

day, the tribal council supervises the use of land on the reservation, assigning tracts for cooperative enterprises, for individuals, and for home builders.

Many of the Ojibwa living in Minnesota came from Michigan's Upper Peninsula and Wisconsin. However, those living at Red Lake Reservation represent a different aspect of the Ojibwa's migration. The Red Lake people came into Minnesota from the north, dislodging the Sioux in the latter half of the 18th century. Their history is linked to other Ojibwa of the Canadian border region, around Rainy River, Lake of the Woods, and the Pembina district of the lower Red River valley.

In their isolated environment, the Ojibwa at Red Lake have preserved the Midewiwin religion, knowledge of herbal medicine, and much of their traditional way of life. Mide leaders persistently opposed the efforts of the government and missionaries to destroy the religious base of their close-knit community. The first Protestant missionaries, who arrived in the 1830s, showed favoritism in distributing gifts rather than treating everyone equally, which was the accepted Indian custom. Red Lake people disapproved and gave the missionaries three years to learn how to behave properly. The missionaries thought that these "pagans" should be grateful for any gifts they received. They failed to change their ways and even hoarded food stores during a winter of shortage instead of sharing with the community. They were forced to leave Red Lake. The next missionaries to come to the reservation arrived in the 1870s. The Ojibwa refused to let them live within the reservation boundaries, so the missionaries settled four miles away. Not until the 1920s were two evangelical missionaries able to gain Christian converts among the more traditional people at the Red Earth Reservation.

The geography of the Red Lake region helped the most traditional people avoid government supervision. The principal community is situated at the end of a long peninsula between the upper and lower lakes. The government agency was built at the site of the present-day town of Red Lake, on the south shore of Lower Red Lake. The 12-mile canoe trip from the south shore to the peninsula was often dangerous, though the crossing was easier in winter, when the lake was frozen. There were few horses, and people avoided the lakeshore path, which was 40 miles long and crossed over numerous streams.

On the peninsula, the surrounding water tempered the climate, creating weather conditions favorable for growing corn, potatoes, squashes, and beans. Here also were tall forests, maple trees, berries, fish, deer, wild rice, and medicinal herbs. Because these basic resources were available, Red Lake people were able to resist government efforts to change them into stock-raising, horse-and-plow farmers.

The federal government continued its attempt to eradicate Ojibwa traditional culture and to replace it with a non-Indian way of life. The BIA devised programs that were supposed to develop the Ojibwa economy and improve housing, health care, and education. In effect, the BIA's civilization program created a people of two worlds. Furthermore, although many of the Ojibwa appeared to embrace a new way of life, in reality they became dependent on the government rather than self-sufficient citizens. In the late 1920s, as the timber industry began to fail, after the virgin forests were completely cut down, the Ojibwa economy weakened, and reservation farmers sold their equipment and stock. In the 1930s, when the Great Depression deepened the economic crisis, the federal government finally realized that a new policy was needed not only toward the Ojibwa but toward all Indians. ▲

Alex Kakapsche, an Ojibwa elder and dancer, with a child at a powwow in Sault Ste. Marie, Michigan. Through dancing, drumming, and storytelling, the modern Ojibwa identify with Anishinabe ancestors and maintain their traditional culture.

THE
MODERN ANISHINABE

The bleak picture of life on White Earth and many other reservations in the 1920s changed in 1933 with the development of President Franklin D. Roosevelt's New Deal. This reform program, enacted in response to the depression that followed the 1929 stock market crash, featured benefits for impoverished citizens, including many Indian people. Under New Deal work programs, Ojibwa received jobs planting trees in reforestation projects. They also helped to build roads, bridges, and fire towers and to string telephone lines through rural areas.

Another related legislation, the Indian Reorganization Act (IRA) of 1934, was designed particularly to aid Indians form their own tribal governments. As part of the Indian New Deal, the IRA was chiefly the creation of John C. Collier, who served as commissioner of Indian affairs from 1933 to 1945. Collier was a great crusader for change in the government's policy toward Indian

people. He ensured that the new Indian program would immediately end the allotment policy, which had caused Indians across the nation to lose their right to their ancestral homelands. New laws returned many acres of unsold land within reservation boundaries to tribal ownership and allowed for the purchase of additional tracts for tribal use. White Earth, Leech Lake, and Red Lake were among the reservations benefiting from these measures.

Collier also helped to put an end to the government's efforts to destroy Indian religion, language, government, and way of life. Under IRA guidelines, tribes could write constitutions and form new representative governing bodies. In addition, tribes were given the option to become incorporated, a measure intended to aid the economic growth of reservation communities.

As a result of the Indian New Deal, the Ojibwa at Fond du Lac, Grand Portage, Bois Forte, White Earth, Leech

Lake, and Mille Lacs organized them-selves into the Minnesota Chippewa Tribe, with headquarters at the town of Cass Lake. Two delegates from each group made up the Tribal Executive Committee, which exercised central governing powers. Each reservation also had its own tribal council that es-tablished business enterprises, ar-ranged loans, and hired lawyers. Red Lake incorporated as a separate tribe.

The right to have legal counsel be-came more important to the Ojibwa after the federal government created the Indian Claims Commission in 1946. The commission was organized to re-solve all grievances that Indian groups had against the United States as a result of past treaties and land cessions. The Ojibwa tribes in Michigan, Wisconsin, and Minnesota went before this body, suing the federal government for mis-management of their lands and funds. Some cases are still pending.

In another revolutionary change of government policy, Collier actually pro-moted the preservation of Indian cul-tures. The commissioner declared that Indian students should become fluent in their own native language as well as in English. This was good news to the Ojibwa parents who, in an effort to pro-tect their children from being punished in government schools, had stopped teaching their children the Ojibwa lan-guage. Collier also believed that Indians should be free to practice their tradi-tional religions and that the songs, dances, legends, and artwork of Indian

people should be preserved and appre-ciated.

Thus, in the 1930s, BIA-employed schoolteachers began studying Indian values. Because the home and com-munity were so important to the Ojib-wa's culture, some boarding schools were closed and more local schools were opened. A curriculum was devel-oped to include instruction in Indian culture, as well as vocational training. Public schools, however, remained in-sensitive to the needs of Native Ameri-cans for the next 30 years.

Despite government assistance dur-ing the Great Depression, the Ojibwa economy faltered. Although most men lacked the skills required for jobs off the reservation, wage work provided much of their income. At Fond du Lac Res-ervation, the estimated average family income dropped to $310, most of which came from wages. A small percentage came from self-employment, including farming, selling forest products, and manufacturing artwork and crafts.

The American involvement in World War II (1941–45) bolstered the Native American economy. On reser-vations throughout the Great Lakes re-gion, the Ojibwa contributed to the war effort by increasing production. Ap-proximately 40,000 American Indians moved to urban centers to work in fac-tories, shipyards, aircraft plants, and railroad yards. Ojibwa laborers worked at the Walter Butler shipyards in Su-perior, Wisconsin. Others from Lac du Flambeau qualified for army and navy

A cabin at Grand Portage, Minnesota, around 1935. Despite government assistance during the Great Depression, the Ojibwa economy faltered and reservation life suffered during this period of national crisis.

wartime construction jobs in Alaska and Newfoundland, Canada. Off-reservation earnings and income generated from military service worked to improve the quality of life on Ojibwa reservations. Relief cases decreased by 50 percent. In addition, the war had a great personal impact on Ojibwa servicemen. Many of those who joined the armed services for the first time had the opportunity to associate with Americans of different cultural groups.

The war years also affected the Ojibwa adversely, as the government provided less money for domestic spending during this time of international crisis. Congress slashed funds appropriated for IRA programs. These cuts led to the physical deterioration of reservation facilities, such as schools, hospitals, roads, and telephone networks. The government also once again began to disregard the importance of both the Indians' cultural heritage and their desire for self-government. The BIA shifted its emphasis from providing a cross-cultural education for rural students to preparing Native Americans for urban life.

In the 1950s, the BIA inaugurated a new policy known as relocation. Through its relocation program, the

When the United States commissioned an artist to paint an individual from each branch of the armed services during World War II, the U.S. Army selected an Ojibwa Indian as its representative. This portrait of bomber pilot Charles Moose, of Mille Lacs, was painted in Pomigliano, Italy, and now hangs in the Pentagon. His plane was named Chippewa Chief.

government urged Indians to leave their somewhat secure reservation life and to migrate to urban areas, such as Chicago, Illinois; Denver, Colorado; and Oakland and Los Angeles, California. BIA officials maintained that as city dwellers Indians would quickly abandon their old ways, join mainstream American society, and improve their economic lot by finding work with non-Indian businesses. Government officials also hoped that by reducing the reservation population, the relocation policy would allow them to cut services and funds owed to Indian tribes.

For more than two decades, Lake Superior Indians were relocated to cities in the Midwest. Almost 12,000 of Minnesota's 22,322 Native Americans were living in urban areas by the mid-1970s. The hope of having a job and a stable income drew them away from impoverished reservations.

At more remote reservations, such as Nett Lake (Bois Forte) and Grand Portage, the Ojibwa were able still to profit from their wildlife resources. In 1958, the sale of fishing and hunting permits alone generated $53,358 at Grand Portage and $68,890 at Nett Lake. However, many Ojibwa depended on finding wage work. For those who refused to relocate to urban areas, the BIA continued its effort to develop the reservation economy. Federal loans encouraged tribal councils to finance individual and cooperative enterprises on the reservation. Bad River extended over $24,000 in credit for seed, livestock, boats, machinery, and

other items between June 1, 1957 and June 30, 1958. With a $35,000 loan from Lac Courte Oreilles in 1962, the Shelton Basket Company at Reserve opened for business and hired 38 Ojibwa. However, residents of Lac Courte Oreilles, much like those at Keweenaw Bay, Mole Lake, Bad River, Red Cliff, Fond du Lac, Grand Portage, and Nett Lake, experienced no substantial cash income from industrial employment.

At the beginning of the 1960s, John Collier's goal to help Indian people become self-sufficient and prosperous had been unfulfilled. IRA programs had taken great steps in this direction, but World War II had created a postwar environment that demanded the integration of Indian populations into the thriving economies of urban areas. However, the presidency of Lyndon B. Johnson (1963–69) marked a turning point for most Indian people. As part of President Johnson's War on Poverty program in the United States, the government established the Office of Economic Opportunity (OEO). Funds from the OEO were set aside for reservation inhabitants to develop their own businesses and social programs. In order to spend the money effectively, tribal councils set up committees to canvass for jobs and to determine community needs in areas such as housing and health care.

With OEO allocations, tribal governments were able to take over functions once performed by the BIA. More and more jobs opened up on the reservations. Indian political leaders became

A 1957 Bureau of Indian Affairs (BIA) photograph of an Ojibwa family outside their house in Waukegan, Illinois. Hoping to cut services and funds due Indians, the U.S. government, in the 1950s, inaugurated a relocation program to urge Indians to leave reservations for job training in urban areas.

skilled reservation administrators and worked together to establish intertribal associations to strengthen their position in dealing with non-Indians.

In the 1970s, the government committed itself to improving education for Indian children by passing the Indian Education Act. The law gave Indian parents and communities a voice in deciding how government funds for schools could best be used. The Indian Self-Determination and Education Assistance Act of 1975 reinforced the United States's commitment to this policy. This act forbade the secretary of the interior from entering into a contract for the education of Indians without consultation of school and parents.

The change in federal policy sparked a new interest in the Ojibwa language and way of life in Minnesota. Traditional education became important in Minneapolis, St. Paul, and Duluth, where a third of the state's Indian population was living by the 1960s. The director of the Indian community center in St. Paul established an alternative school offering language classes. Because of this program, the school day for many of the Ojibwa students begins with the recitation of prayers in the Ojibwa language accompanied by the ceremonial burning of tobacco.

Tribal councils on Ojibwa reservations provided scholarships for hundreds of promising high school graduates to attend universities and trade schools. The state of Minnesota appropriated $140,000 in 1973 and $230,000 in 1974 to help Indians attend college. The Department of American Indian Studies at the University of Minnesota at Minneapolis St. Paul provides counselors, tutors, and instruction in the Ojibwa and Sioux languages. There are Native American programs at campuses in the University of Wisconsin system. A special division at Michigan State University in East Lansing, Michigan, promotes similar objectives. The Bay Mills Reservation west of Sault Ste. Marie has established its own community college. Legislation enables Indian students in Michigan to attend state institutions without paying tuition.

The Ojibwa have indeed come to value education. Dropout rates declined significantly in the 1970s at many reservations. Parents are not only involved in their children's education. Many of them attend nearby colleges or adult education classes on their reservation. Tribal council members recognize that education will help solve many problems, such as economic underdevelopment, experienced by Indians.

In general, education programs have generated increased pride and in-

terest in the Ojibwa culture. Author and scholar Gerald Vizenor, who grew up at White Earth, has used material recovered from old issues of the reservation newspaper, the *Tomahawk*, in some of his own work. Another Ojibwa writer, John Rodgers, has published his recollections of his schooling at White Earth. Preserving literature in the Ojibwa language, Maude Kegg of Mille Lacs Reservation recorded legends that have been published in Ojibwa and En-

Three Head Start graduates at White Earth Reservation. A War on Poverty program initiated in 1965, Head Start provides disadvantaged preschoolers with an environment that nurtures social competence and learning. At the four Head Start centers on White Earth, children learn the Ojibwa language, hear stories, and participate in an annual powwow.

Maude Kegg, of Mille Lacs Reservation, displaying some of her beadwork. In addition to keeping a traditional Ojibwa craft alive, she has published two books on Ojibwa legends, for which she received the National Heritage Award in 1990.

glish. For her work, she received a National Heritage Award in 1990 from the National Foundation for the Arts.

The Ojibwa today are far from being a homogeneous group. Communities are widely dispersed and differ economically and culturally. However, elements of traditional culture, such as language, supernatural beliefs, oral literature, and handicrafts, are still to be found among the Ojibwa. In addition, many continue to fish, hunt, and gather rice. The Ojibwa at Lac du Flambeau, a 40,000-acre reservation with 126 lakes, maintain a trout pond and a fish hatchery that has produced an estimated 300 million fry (small fish) during the past 50 years. Non-Indians, too, are welcome to fish on the reservation lakes.

The Ojibwa at Lac du Flambeau engage in spearfishing every spring, a traditional enterprise that defies the regulations of the Wisconsin Department of Natural Resources. A controversy over spearfishing began in 1974 at Lac Courte Oreilles, when state officials arrested two Indian fishermen. Other Ojibwa reservations joined in the subsequent lawsuit asserting tribal rights to hunt, fish, gather wild rice, and cut timber on all the land they ceded to the United States by treaties in 1837 and 1842.

A small but well-organized group of non-Indian extremists organized demonstrations after a federal district court judge ruled in 1983 that the Indian rights under treaties with the United States are far-reaching and take precedence over the rights of non-Indians to the natural resources. This important ruling, known as the Voigt Decision, also stated that tribal councils have the responsibility to regulate Indian fishing with regard to health, safety, and conservation. Consequently, 13 of the Ojibwa's reservations in Michigan, Wisconsin, and Minnesota joined in creating the Great Lakes Indian Fish and Wildlife Commission (GLIFWC). In compliance with the Wisconsin Department of Natural Resources, they maintain fish hatcheries, hire game wardens, and keep records of every fish that is caught. The GLIFWC staff claims to operate the most carefully controlled fishery in the world.

In the aftermath of the Voigt Decision, the Lac du Flambeau Reservation became the scene of dangerous confrontations. In opposition to Indian spearfishing, a group of non-Indian extremists formed Protect America's Rights and Resources (PARR) and Stop Treaty Abuse (STA). Investigators discovered that these organizations had outside support from white supremacist groups. Traditional spearers of the tribe joined forces as members of the Wa-Swa-Gon Association. Their name in the native language means "Lake of the Torches," translated by the French as "Lac du Flambeau." It refers to the custom of nighttime fishing using flaming cedar torches to locate fish for spearing. In the spring of 1989 and 1990, Ojibwa fishermen suffered physical attacks, survived a bomb placed at a boat landing, and endured having their fishing boats capsized by anchors trailing

THE TIES THAT BIND

Like their relatives in the United States, Canadian Ojibwa maintain an Anishinabe heritage through councils, powwows, and other ceremonies. They also continue to fish and to gather wild rice. These activities serve to strengthen ties among various, distant communities. Ojibwa who live north of the rice-growing lakes in Canada travel hundreds of miles to share in fall harvests. They also continue to reap the rice by hand, believing that it is a gift from the Creator. Because the Ojibwa in both Canada and the United States share this belief, they have joined to protest the mechanical harvesting of rice by non-Indians.

Maintaining this network of contact among the Ojibwa involves many people. Of the approximately 200,000 Ojibwas in the world today, about two-thirds are Canadian. Although they reside in major cities such as Toronto and Winnipeg and in communities that are not officially recognized by the government, the Ojibwa still make their home on the many reserves scattered throughout the provinces of Ontario, Manitoba, and Saskatchewan. Like American Ojibwa, they were forced to live on reserves after ceding their land to government officials.

In the 1830s, the British government in present-day Canada initiated a "civilization" program, with the objective of reserving land on which Indians could settle and learn to farm. Although an experimental reserve at Coldwater on Lake Simcoe failed in 1837, the reserve system extended throughout the Great Lakes region. By 1850, the Ojibwa received a number of small reserves in Ontario. Those now living at Garden River, Ontario, are direct descendants of the Ojibwa who were settled along the St. Marys River 500 years ago.

The most western Ojibwa reserves are in Saskatchewan. There are as many as a dozen near the city of North Battleford alone. Another eight reserves in the province, as well as a few in Alberta, combine Ojibwa and Cree populations. In Manitoba, the Ojibwa living east of Lake Winnipeg received six shoreline reserves between the Winnipeg and Poplar rivers after surrendering their land in 1875. Other reserves are located upstream on inland lakes, but the Poplar River represents the approximate edge of Ojibwa expansion north of Lake Superior in the 19th century. Beyond it lie reserves for people of mixed Ojibwa and Cree heritage, who call themselves Oji-Crees.

Southeast of Lake Winnipeg and north of the city of Kenora, more than 24 reserves are located on the upper Winnipeg River and on Lake of the Woods. These reserves were established through a treaty signed in 1873 by 24 leaders representing bands living on the Canadian shores of the lake as well as on Rainy River and Rainy Lake. Bands who later signed the treaty lived north of Lake Nipigon and as far east as Mille Lacs, toward Thunder Bay. The Ojibwa of the Thunder Bay area belong to the Fort William band, named after the British post located about 10 miles up the Kaministikwia River.

The band leaders of the Boundary Waters, who met for the 1873 treaty councils, differed from most Ojibwa dealing with Canadian officials. They understood how to bargain with government officials because they had consulted Minnesota kinfolk who had already signed treaties with the United States. Furthermore, unlike most Ojibwa, they actually wanted to farm the land, for they lived in a climate favorable to agriculture and had already become skilled gardeners. They signed the treaty only when the Canadian government agreed to provide livestock, seeds for grain crops, tools for farming and carpentry, and twine for fishnets. Two years later, the Canadian government appended to this treaty a provision for a "half-breed" band, whose leader had been the interpreter at the earlier council. This is the only "half-breed" band included in a Canadian treaty.

Although the Boundary Waters Ojibwa made a promising start, agriculture soon deteriorated on their reserves. The government sent them defective tools and an improper type of seed. Also, dam building at Kenora raised the water level at Lake of the Woods, covering gardens and hay fields. Then, after Canada passed laws in the 1880s preventing Ojibwa from selling crops outside the reserves, the young men refused to take up farming.

Government bureaucracy has continued to plague the Ojibwa. In the 1970s, the Canadian government hindered Ojibwa plans to market wild rice through a cooperative of growers in Manitoba, Ontario, and Minnesota. To deal more effectively with such problems, Ojibwa and Ottawa leaders from Canada and the United States met in 1990 in a joint conference at the headquarters for the Sault Ste. Marie Tribe of Chippewa Indians, the fourth largest tribe of Indians in the United States. In recognition of their shared heritage, the Canadian Ojibwa presented their American hosts with gifts of blankets and tobacco, the sacred plant, before any discussion could proceed. The ties that bind the Ojibwa are clearly born not only of necessity but of tradition.

behind the powerful motorboats of PARR and STA members. Indian women, too, suffered verbal abuse and hate-inspired slogans.

Controversy over Ojibwa fishing rights has occurred in other states as well as Wisconsin. A similar incident had occurred in Michigan, after a resident of Bay Mills Reservation on Whitefish Bay challenged the rights of the state authorities to control Ojibwa fishing in 1972. Indian fishing rights, stemming from an 1836 treaty, were affirmed in federal district court in 1981. Regional anti-Indian opposition followed but failed to receive as much publicity nationally as it later did in Wisconsin.

Although Lac Courte Oreilles enjoys a cooperative relationship with the local business community, the fishing controversy has hurt the reservation economically. For instance, financial support has diminished for Lac

Two wild ricers on Lower Rice Lake, at White Earth Reservation. Although the Ojibwa people living in the United States and Canada are separated politically, they identify with one another through an Anishinabe heritage, which includes gathering rice, fishing, and hunting.

Courte's radio station (WOJB), the only tribally owned public radio station east of the Mississippi River. With an 80-mile signal, WOJB serves a large area with a variety of programming that includes Indian news and music.

After valuable rice lands were flooded by the U.S. Army Corps of Engineers in 1921, Ojibwa leaders at Lac Courte Oreilles adopted a practical strategy for dealing with the federal government and other non-Indian organizations. Representatives of the Lac Courte Oreilles band and the business community at nearby Hayward joined in forming a corporation in 1989 to promote economic development that would protect natural resources. Carrying out this objective, the tribal chairman traveled to England in 1990 to protest plans of a British firm to exploit the vanadium deposits on the Lac Courte Oreilles Reservation. Tribal councils play a vital role in designing programs to preserve Ojibwa culture, improve health and education, aid the elders of the community, and develop the reservation economy.

The Ojibwa, like other Indians in the United States and Canada, are striving to maintain an identity independent of non-Indians. This identity includes a historical tradition that precedes contact with whites and, though changed through time, remains vital today. The Ojibwa continue to maintain their varied heritage through storytelling, art, councils, and powwows. In ceremonies, dancing, and drumming, they are still Anishinabe. ▲

BIBLIOGRAPHY

Blackbird, Andrew (Chief Mack-aw-de-be-nessy). *History of the Ottawa and Chippewa Indians of Michigan: A Grammar of the Language and Personal and Family History of the Author, by Andrew J. Blackbird, Late U.S. Interpreter*. 1887. Reprint. Petoskey, MI: Little Traverse Regional Historical Society, 1967.

Danziger, Edmund Jefferson, Jr. *The Chippewas of Lake Superior*. Norman: University of Oklahoma Press, 1979.

Henry, Alexander. *Travels and Adventures in Canada and the Indian Territories Between the Years 1760 and 1776*. 1809 Reprint. Edmonton, Alberta: Hurtig, 1969.

Johnston, Basil. *Ojibway Ceremonies*. Lincoln: University of Nebraska Press, 1990.

———. *The Ojibwa Heritage*. Toronto: McClelland and Stewart; New York: Columbia University Press, 1976.

Smith, Donald B. *The Reverend Peter Jones (Kahkewaguonaby) and the Missisauga Indians*. Lincoln: University of Nebraska Press, 1987.

Tanner, Helen Hornbeck, ed. *Atlas of Great Lakes Indian History*. Norman: University of Oklahoma Press, 1987.

Tanner, John. *A Narrative of the Captivity and Adventures of John Tanner (U.S. Interpreter at the Saut de Ste. Maria) During Thirty Years Residence Among the Indians in the Interior of North America*. Edited by Edwin James. 1830. Reprint. Minneapolis: Ross and Haines, 1956.

Warren, William Whipple. *History of the Ojibway People*. St. Paul: Minnesota Historial Society Press, 1984.

THE OJIBWA AT A GLANCE

TRIBE   *Ojibwa*

CULTURE AREA   *Great Lakes*

GEOGRAPHY   *The Ojibwa migrated from the Atlantic coast more than 500 years ago and settled in the region around the eastern end of Lake Superior and the north shore of Lake Huron. After 200 years of expansion, the Ojibwa now live on more than 100 reservations and reserves and in communities in Michigan, Wisconsin, Minnesota, North Dakota, and Montana and in the Canadian provinces of Ontario, Manitoba, and Saskatchewan. Many other Ojibwa live in cities or in communities that are not officially recognized.*

LINGUISTIC FAMILY   *Algonquian*

CURRENT POPULATION   *Approximately 200,000*

FIRST CONTACT   *French traders in early 17th century*

FEDERAL STATUS   *In the United States, 15 tribal organizations are recognized and 3 more Ojibwa-Ottawa bands are in the process of applying for federal acknowledgment. Approximately 70 bands have federal status in Canada.*

agent A person appointed by the Bureau of Indian Affairs to supervise U.S. government programs on a reservation and/or in a specific region.

Algonkian The Indian peoples living in the northeastern United States and east-central Canada whose languages are related and who share numerous cultural characteristics.

Algonquian The languages spoken by most Indian peoples in northeastern North America.

allotment U.S. policy applied nationwide through the General Allotment Act of 1887, aimed at breaking up tribally owned reservations by assigning individual farms and ranches to Indians. Allotment was intended as much to discourage traditional communal activities as to encourage private farming and assimilate Indians into mainstream American life.

annuity Compensation for land and/or resources based on terms of a treaty or other agreement between the United States and an individual tribe. Annuities consisted of goods, services, and cash given to the tribe every year for a specified period.

assimilation The complete absorption of one group into another group's cultural tradition.

band A loosely organized group of people who are bound together by the need for food and defense, by family ties, and/or by other common interests.

Bureau of Indian Affairs (BIA) A U.S. government agency now within the Department of the Interior. Originally intended to manage trade and other relations with Indians, the BIA today seeks to develop and implement programs that encourage Indians to manage their own affairs and to improve their educational opportunities and general social and economic well-being.

civilization program U.S. policy of the late 19th and early 20th centuries designed to change the Indians' way of life so that it resembled that of non-Indians. These programs usually focused on converting Indians to Christianity and encouraging them to become farmers.

clan A multigenerational group having a shared identity, organization, and property based on belief in their descent from a common ancestor. Because clan members consider themselves closely related, marriage within a clan is strictly prohibited.

culture The learned behavior of humans; nonbiological, socially taught activities; the way of life of a group of people.

fur trade Trading network in North America through which Indians gave Europeans animal pelts in exchange for manufactured goods.

Indian New Deal Program inaugurated by the Indian Reorganization (Wheeler-Howard) Act of 1934, designed to remove government restrictions on Indian traditions and to encourage autonomous development of Indian communities.

Indian Reorganization Act The 1934 federal law that ended the policy of allotting plots of land to individuals and encouraged the development of reservation communities. Also, the act provided for the creation of autonomous tribal governments.

lineage A group of individuals related through descent from a common ancestor; a descent group whose members recognize as relatives people on the mother's side only or the father's side only.

Midewiwin An Ojibwa medicine society in which the Mide (medicine men and women) used plants, prayers, and song in their curing ceremonies.

mission A religious center founded by advocates of a particular denomination who are trying to convert nonbelievers to their faith.

missionaries Advocates of a particular religion who travel to convert nonbelievers to their faith.

nation A term used generally by the early Europeans in North America to describe the Indian tribal societies they encountered. Broadly, any large group of people having similar institutions, language, customs, and political and social ties.

powwow An Indian social gathering that includes feasting, dancing, rituals, and arts and crafts displays, to which other Indian groups as well as non-Indians are now often invited.

removal policy A federal policy of the early 19th century that called for the sale of all Indian land in the eastern United States and the migration of Indians from these areas to lands west of the Mississippi River.

reservation, reserve A tract of land retained by Indians for their own occupation and use. *Reser-*

vation is used to describe such lands in the United States; *reserve*, in Canada.

totem The emblem or symbol of a clan or family, usually the animal or plant that the family claims as its mythical ancestor.

treaty A contract negotiated between representatives of the U.S. government or another national government and one or more Indian tribes. Treaties dealt with the cessation of military action, the surrender of political independence, the es-tablishment of boundaries, terms of land sales, and related matters.

tribe A society consisting of several or many separate communities united by kinship, culture, language, and other social institutions including clans, religious organizations, and warrior societies.

wigwam A low, dome-shaped lodging constructed from a frame of living saplings and from mats of cedar or birch bark, which were placed on top of the frame to form the walls and roof.

PICTURE CREDITS

American Museum of Natural History, pages 22 (neg. # 312292), 23 (neg. # 315506), 25 (neg. # 320374); The Bettmann Archive, pages 32, 39, 40, 48, 50, 56, 68, 70, 71; Culver Pictures, pages 37, 53; Courtesy of C.J. Hambleton Collection, photo by Helen Hombeck Tanner, page 75; Library of Congress, pages 36, 42, 74; From the collection of the Minnesota Historical Society, pages 15 ([E97.37, r85] St. Paul Dispatch Photo), 28 ([E97.37, r48] Robert G. Beaulieu, photographer), 89 (E97.37, r71), 90 (E97.7w, p24), 93 (E97.71, p10), 96 (E97.4, p9), 101 ([E97.76, p7] Monroe Kelly, photographer); National Archives, pages 94, 104; The Newberry Library, pages 12, 16, 20, 24, 26, 29, 35, 66, 72, 81; Courtesy of Phil J. Newkumet, page 102; Win Awenen Nistotung, page 98; Photo by Edward Owen, courtesy of Department of Anthropology, Smithsonian Institution, cover (cat. # 175281), pages 57 (cat. # 338881), 58 (top [cat. # 307104], bottom [cat. # 287644]), 59 (cat. # 307104), 60 (left [cat. # 175286], right [cat. # 153036]), 61 (left [cat. # 326124], right [cat. # 328762]), 62 (top [cat. # 377745], bottom [cat. # 416198]), 63 (cat. # 287645), 64 (cat. # 338834); Courtesy of the St. Louis County Historical Society, page 84 (E97.7g, p4); *Star Tribune*, Minneapolis, MN. Photo by Zerby, page 106; State Historical Society of Wisconsin, pages 30–31, 82, 85; White Earth Reservation, pages 105, 110.

Maps (pages 2, 18, 46–47, 54–55, 76–77, 86–87) by Gary Tong.

HELEN HORNBECK TANNER, who received her Ph.D. in history from the University of Michigan, is a research associate at the Newberry Library. She is the author of *The Ojibwas: A Critical Bibliography* and the editor of *Atlas of Great Lakes Indian History*. She has served as an expert witness in cases presented before the Indian Claims Commission and as historical consultant in other legal cases concerning Indian treaties.

FRANK W. PORTER III, general editor of INDIANS OF NORTH AMERICA, is director of the Chelsea House Foundation for American Indian Studies. He holds a B.A., M.A., and Ph.D. from the University of Maryland. He has done extensive research concerning the Indians of Maryland and Delaware and is the author of numerous articles on their history, archaeology, geography, and ethnography. He was formerly director of the Maryland Commission on Indian Affairs and American Indian Research and Resource Institute, Gettysburg, Pennsylvania, and he has received grants from the Delaware Humanities Forum, the Maryland Committee for the Humanities, the Ford Foundation, and the National Endowment for the Humanities, among others. Dr. Porter is the author of *The Bureau of Indian Affairs* in the Chelsea House KNOW YOUR GOVERNMENT series.